All God's Children

JOURNEYS IN FAITH

Speech, Silence, Action! The Cycle of Faith
Virginia Ramey Mollenkott

Creative Dislocation—The Movement of Grace
Robert McAfee Brown

Hope Is an Open Door
Mary Luke Tobin

By Way of Response
Martin E. Marty

Ten Commandments for the Long Haul
Daniel Berrigan

God's Presence in My Life
Edward W. Bauman

Disputed Questions: On Being a Christian
Rosemary Radford Ruether

All God's Children

Tilden Edwards

Journeys in Faith
Robert A. Raines, Editor

ABINGDON
Nashville

ALL GOD'S CHILDREN
Copyright © 1982 by Abingdon

Library of Congress Cataloging in Publication Data

EDWARDS, TILDEN.
All God's children.
(Journeys in faith)
1. Edwards, Tilden H., 1935– . 2. Episcopal Church—
Clergy—Biography. 3. Clergy—United States—Biography.
I. Title. II. Series.
BX5995.E46A3 283'.3 [B] 81-12704 AACR2

ISBN 0-687-01016-0

MANUFACTURED BY THE PARTHENON PRESS AT
NASHVILLE, TENNESSEE, UNITED STATES OF AMERICA

*For my children Jeremy and Jennifer,
that they may know and delight in
the One who guides them along the
Way—through all things.*

Contents

Editor's Foreword

People inside and outside the church today are engaged in a profound revisioning of the faith journey. Wanting to honor our own heritage and to be nourished by our roots, we also want to discern the signs of the kingdom now, and to move into the 1980s with a lean, biblical, ecumenical and human faith perspective.

The Journeys in Faith book series is offered to facilitate this revisioning of faith. Reflecting on the social justice openings of the 1960s and the inward searching of the 1970s, these books articulate a fresh integration of the faith journey for the years ahead. They are personal and social. Authors have been invited to share what has been happening to them in their faith and life in recent years, and then to focus on issues which have become primary for them in this time.

We believe that these lucidly written books will be widely used by study groups in congregations, seminaries, colleges, renewal centers, orders, and denominations, as well as for personal study and reflection.

Our distinguished authors embody a diversity of experience and perspective which will provide many points of identification and enrichment for readers. As we enter into the pilgrimages shared in these books we will find resonance, encouragement, and insight for a fresh appropriation of our faith, toward personal and social transformation.

Tilden Edwards brings a rare interfaith heritage and experience to the Journeys in Faith series. Welsh by naming, he grew up as a Roman Catholic in Texas, Manhattan, and the West Coast, eventually becoming an Episcopal priest. Over a period of sixteen years in Washington, D.C. he served an urban parish, became the director of an interfaith center for the training of clergy and laity (spent a sabbatical in a Buddhist center) and created the Shalem Institute for Spiritual Formation. He is as he puts it, a "true-blue cross-fertilized American," with six ethnic heritages coursing through him. This rich gathering of truth from many sources has deepened and gentled the center stream of his own profoundly Christian faith.

"Fidelity to place" is a reality and theme of his pilgrimage. Washington, D.C. is the place. Over a period of sixteen years in that city he shared in a team ministry at St. Stephen and the Incarnation, a congregation committed to serving the poor and a center of the civil rights and anti-Vietnam war movements of the 1960s and early 1970s. After five years immersed in this parish and its neighborhood people, he became director of the Metropolitan Ecumenical Training Center, an interfaith organization training clergy and lay leadership for varieties of ministries in the metropolitan area. Tilden created the Shalem Institute for Spiritual Formation in 1976. While personally still grounded in the justice and peace concerns of his previous involvements, Shalem has been developed as a center for spiritual pilgrimage, working as a bridge institution, interfacing theological, contemplative, and psychological perspectives in the development of a program of spiritual guidance and friendship, among many other offerings.

Tilden shares the pilgrimage of his family life through these years, including the learnings of a stint of communal living in the St. Stephen's years, learning about the need for privacy as well as intimacy.

Through it all we see a man struggling with "a personal success drive in tension with the larger social-religious vision," a tension many of us readers will recognize in our own journeys. There is a sense of balance and personal ease in this man, a man comfortable with his being, whose life is integrating its various components towards "reality as a co-inherent whole." He is a healthy holy man. A gentle and true guide for the pilgrimage.

This is a book about congregational life and mission, about ministry for clergy and laity. It will make an excellent handbook for congregational and denominational leaders seeking a clear mirror to reflect faithful styles of Christian witness in the years ahead. This is for those concerned with the ongoing transformation of faithful congregations and Christians. It is a comforting, healing, and encouraging book.

Robert A. Raines

1

Whose Journey?

My personal journey is no more "special" a journey than yours or anyone else's. Each of us is called to participate uniquely in the joy, brokenness, and caring of this life. But we can share with one another, and we can realize our solidarity in a common journey and moments of "arrival" that speak to the very fluid boundaries between us in the one Body. We can recognize ourselves, be warned and comforted, and in our own way illumined by another's story. It is in that spirit that I offer you these episodes from a very unheroic, ordinary life, yet one privileged to be positioned at times to experience a rich variety of people, places, and events.

I will portray my journey primarily in terms of spiritual discernment, so far as I am able. I will look for the ways God seems to have sounded through our times and in my life.

It is not easy to discern these ways in which God comes through our lives. Paul makes this clear when he exclaims, "O the depth of the riches and wisdom and knowledge of God! How unsearchable are his judgments and how inscrutable his ways!" (Rom. 11:33).

At the same time Paul doesn't let this awareness stop him from trying! These words follow several chapters of joining his God-given experience, faith, reason, and intuition into a discernment of God's ways with Israel.

In that same chapter of Romans Paul also says, "All that exists comes from [God]; all is by him and for him" (11:36 JB). Thus our whole lives in a sense are grace notes, played by and in God. Even the sinful, painful times of "outsideness" that our freedom in God allows can be in time mysteriously turned inside out by God, transformed from dissonance to harmony. And yet such outsideness has a way of delaying the kingdom. Distortion breeds distortion, the sins of the fathers and mothers are visited on the sons and daughters to a fourth generation—and beyond. We are called to heed the ways grace would hasten the time when "God will be all in all."

So it is to that mysterious current of grace I will try to attend in these pages. My hope is that as we each attend God's grace in and around us, we will live ever more fully out of the Heart that would pace our lives and awaken us for our continuing part in the one journey.

God's grace is a mystery—half hidden and half revealed. We cannot solve God's mystery in our lives, but we can appreciate it, with open minds and hearts, and with the aid of those graced before us and among us, in scripture, tradition, and the ever-expanding communion of saints.

Whose journey is it that I describe? I am called priest, father, husband, friend, citizen, Tilden, and many other names. Who is the real me? The answer is that nobody knows our real name except God; that awareness, it has been said, saves us from being slave to any of the names others give us, even to names we give ourselves.

In Genesis we are empowered to name animals and

plants, but only God can name *us*. God names us loved and free, sons and daughters of divine mystery.

If we cling to our own more particular name, title, role, position too tightly, we turn ourselves into a finite, hard idol that we subtly worship. The ego-centered individualism of recent culture feeds this idol. Then we no longer journey in liberating faith, but in oppressive, passive idolatry.

Such a hard, presumedly isolated, centripetal self is a confused, willful illusion that must die, is empowered to die, on the cross. What is left then is what Thomas Merton calls a "graced nothing." A self dead and risen with Christ is "no thing" in *itself:* that person realizes such a co-inherence with God and creation that nothing can possibly subsist independently of the whole. Yet this self is a *graced* nothing, and therefore a relative *something:* relative to God, relative of God: a marvelous, unique, meant to be, vibrant, gifted yet incomplete cell of God's endless Body.

2

Preparation: Mongrel Nomad

Inheritance

Standing on a hill in south Wales last summer I surveyed the ancient, green hills of the land that bore my great grandfather. No visible trace of Welsh custom remained in my family. And yet I carried a Welsh name. I knew a little of the intuitive, incarnate spirituality still alive in Welsh poetry, stories, and music, brought forward over a thousand years (and who knows from how much farther back) from Celtic Christian spirituality.

Donald Allchin, a canon of Canterbury Cathedral, though not Welsh himself, is a "convert" to the importance and rarity of that neglected spirituality in the English-speaking world. In reading and talking with him, I was doubly moved toward those hills.

My time there was far too short and hectic. But the Spirit at times still seemed to reach me. I learned of fidelity to graced places. Holy places are important in Celtic spirituality: holy wells, churches, cemeteries, saints' dwellings. This need not be the idolatry of "God in a box": God restricted to place. Rather, it can be the sacramentality of a special place: a sign of divine presence that gives us hope and eyes to see the glory of God everywhere.

Some of these obscure rural churches and holy wells have been in continuous use for thirteen hundred years. People near them trusted that a place where there was visible experience of divine healing and wise loving would remain such for others. A place where once the veil between heaven and earth was thinned would continue to provide a particular transparency for yearning mortals. So these places are kept sacred, not as historical monuments, but as living windows for an eternal light.

I yielded to this subtle power of place as I washed my face in the hidden holy well of St. Issui at Patrishow. Beside me was James Coutes, an Anglican priest from Brecon, who embodied fidelity to place in the most authentic way. As he took me from one holy place to another, he never failed to connect it with all of life's holiness everywhere. At the well he spoke of its power within us all, quoting Ignatius of Antioch, who "felt a spring of water in his heart rising from the Father." Once he stopped in the middle of what seemed nowhere, took me up a grassy hill crisp with a sharp breeze, and put into my hand a poem by the contemporary Welsh Christian poet, R. S. Thomas, which speaks of the wind crumbling over us like bread.

James' sense of place undergirds his life as a parish priest. A priest, he said, celebrates Eucharist and blesses the authentic events of life, watching for transformation. A priest, like a father or mother, allows space for his people to grow, and then dies there in their midst. Fidelity to place. Here is a lesson for all us too restless, striving Americans.

Thomas Merton, of partial Welsh ancestry himself, once said that we are all destined to continue the histories of our ancestors. Each of us carries forward, consciously or unconsciously, the sins, struggles, and dreams of those whose genes we bear. The death of each generation has a benevolent potential for cleansing us from what has been too tightly held by those who came before. Yet our ancestors were a kind of "holy place," too, who bore signs of the Spirit's opening presence. When we return to them, we need to attend to the lessons of their sins and of their blessedness. Their time is not ours. And yet we bring to our own unique time the same temptations and courage.

In ignoring the experience of our forebears we miss our longer "biography," through which we see both our blindness and our hope. So many of us have the added genetic and cultural strength of "cross-fertilization" ethnically. And yet some of the strength is sapped in our ignorance of detail. That is the drive behind the quest for "roots," brought to a particular intensity in recent years, but a perennial quest in us somewhere. The danger is not going deep enough. I cannot stop with my ethnic identity, or I will end with but one more idol. That identity at best is a larger window through which I can sense more fully the play and sacrifice of God running through our common life.

I am a true-blue, cross-fertilized American. Six ethnic heritages course through me. Like so many others, I know little about my ancestors, except those I have known personally. From what I know they all came to this country for the usual reasons: to escape political, social, and economic oppression and to "make it" in these same areas for themselves and their families in a new land. For many Americans who have come over in the last century and a half, religion, I think, "just came along for the ride." It often was important, especially for the first two generations, but people did not come primarily out of religious or communal motivation. They came for personal gain.

My great grandfather cut through this pattern a bit in the political arena, or at least a family legend would have it so. During the Hayes-Tilden presidential race in 1876 he seems to have been running for sheriff in Lexington, Kentucky, a strong supporter of the reform-minded Tilden ticket. When Tilden lost the election, so the story goes, so did he; he was shot out of town in a classic hotel gun battle by a local corrupt political gang and moved to Fayette, Missouri. He named his son Tilden after his political hero, giving him the middle name of "Hampton," after the then governor of Missouri, another hero of my great grandfather. I am the third Tilden Hampton, branded with the political reformist names of an earlier era. Though these names do not carry the full religious vision that I might wish, at least they keep me mindful of an immigrant ancestor who saw his "personal gain" in publicly concerned terms.

I have dwelt on ancestry because I think it affects our values more than we are prone to think. My family has aimed me in the same direction toward which they were driven in coming: toward an individual and family freedom and accomplishment, sporadically translated into social and religious concern.

Every social and religious vision in this country must come to terms with this personal drive for personal gain. It is a drive that seems to be our American gift, and yet it easily is corrupted into our curse. This happens whenever it is cut off from a transcendent communal vision for life. Then power, money, relationships, and skill are turned to lethal private focus, through which we can lose our souls. These relative means are turned into ultimate ends around which our identities freeze. They lose their potential as sacraments of a larger belonging and turn into self-securing (and ultimately self-destroying) idols.

This relationship of personal drive to a larger social-religious vision is a struggle that has marked my life. That sense of myself as a "graced nothing" and of reality as a "co-inherent whole," expressed in the last chapter, is a recent resolution behind which there has been enormous resistance: in myself and in the conditioning forces of my life. This resistance betrays a belief in a concocted something, not a graced nothing; in closed, protected castles, not a co-inherent whole. Perhaps the struggle between these is basic to the American character today. If so, then much of the world's political destiny rests on its resolution, to the extent that American power affects the world.

That struggle came to maturity for me in the 1960s and 70s, and I will give attention to those years shortly. First, though, I will sketch for you some more of the personal ingredients that I brought into the sixties.

Moving Out

Immigration to this country does not end geographical wandering for millions of Americans. Certainly it did not for me. Before I was born members of my extended family were scattered all over the continent. My parents continued the upheavals: partly voluntary, partly forced by war, employment opportunities, and family circumstances. By the time I reached high school, we had lived in nine cities in Texas, New York, Oregon, and California, with long summer stays with my aunt and uncle in Illinois. These moves involved enormous strain and sense of loss. No place had time to develop a fully rooted quality.

Whenever I read Jesus' warning of hardship to the scribe who promises to follow him—"Foxes have holes, and birds of the air have nests; but the son of man has nowhere to lay his head" (Matt. 8:20)—I think of how many Americans can at least partially identify with such a statement. I always had a nice place to lay my head, but it rarely felt like a full home.

Despite the pain and scars of those moves, I know there was a graced edge to them. They made me aware of the enormous diversity of places and people that inhabit this land. We lived in ethnic communities, inner cities, blue-collar neighborhoods, and middle-class suburbs, in big cities and small towns, with occasional visits to a great uncle's farm. As a result, I feel able to empathize with a great variety of people's living situations.

It seems as though all those years were preparation for living in Washington, D.C., which is such a mishmash of refugees from every corner of the country—and the world. My work, travel, and study in Japan, Latin America, Europe, and Israel have made me feel even more at home in this international city—and home it has been for sixteen years now. Most of this time has been spent in the same neighborhood, one that is right in the middle of the most mixed-up, pulsating, tragic-beautiful section of the city, Adams Morgan. At last, a place! A real home! A place and a time of stability in the eye of the turbulent national hurricane.

That stability has been graced as well. It is as though the Lord wanted me to stay put for a good, long time so that I could attend steadily to my vocation of family and work and not be tempted or forced to spend too much time on my own logistics and orientation.

Through all those years of moving one of the fine

graces given me was a few very close friends. When I left New York City at the age of ten, I took two close friends with me in my heart: David and Sigrid, with whom I maintained a long correspondence and occasional visits. The same has been true with a few friends from high school and graduate school, and new ones made since coming to Washington. I have written about the importance, quality, and neglect of friendship elsewhere. Here I simply want to point out how vital it has been in my often disrupted "placement" to maintain a few friends with whom the intimacy of life's joys, dilemmas, speculations, frustrations, and dreams can be openly and fearlessly shared.

It is worth remembering through all of this that in the end we *all* share Jesus' situation. We have no place ultimately to rest our head, except on the Lord's heart. Yet it is nice to have a human place once in a while that reminds us of that stable yet dynamic core of our lives. Place can become an idol. But it is meant to be a sacrament: an empowering window through which we see not an exclusive center of God, but a sign of that center being everywhere. With that realization, we have our real home with us wherever we are.

Moving Up

"Moving up" usually implies social mobility: moving toward the promised land of social status in the eyes of others. Here, though, I mean another kind of mobility: moving toward the promised land that nobody knows ahead of time, the land toward which Abraham was beckoned in faith, that inner and outer land vibrant with awareness of a deeper self and calling in God.

How have we been supported and encouraged on the way to that land? How has our intrinsic seed of faith been watered—and stunted? So much of our answer rests in endless little events of daily life: how we came to trust our parents and others (or not) through their ways of being trustworthy, how we have been treated, and how it all has been interpreted for us, and by us.

For me, the formal, religious filter was Roman Catholic tradition, reinforced by three years of parochial school in a tough, immigrant-family school in Lower Manhattan (which I entered in the third grade with a branding Texas accent and southern manners). There I was formed in that full, awesome, wondrous, rigid, seemingly unbreakable way of life known as Pre-Vatican II Catholic. Endless masses, novenas, nuns, priests, statues, votive lights, rosaries, confessions, and absolute clarity about right and wrong, true and false, and Irish and Italian.

For all its folk-level character and intimidation, there was something very strong and durable about those years—a strong conditioning in the "law" as teacher, in personal responsibility, and in an awareness of a mysterious reality greater than myself which seeps through all things in judgment and promise. The world was full of holy, spooky places, Catholic solidarity, and divine commands. There was no question of any strictly "private drive" through such a world.

As my parents drifted apart in different personal and religious directions after we moved from New York, I was basically left on my own religiously. I attended mass regularly until college at Stanford, when it all just finally died for me. Ultimate truth there came clothed in behavioral science dress. Each new psychology or anthropology text came as a revelation of the "way things really were."

There was an incompleteness in all the behavioral sciences, though, that led me to make friends with

Quakers, chaplains, and others in the church. In my senior year my vocational tests showed that my personality traits combined what was right for a minister (except that I didn't believe in God)! Something very deep but unknown did stir me that last year, something gave me a hunger so deep that nothing finitely human could satisfy it. There was nothing behind the hunger that I could see then.

I spent the summer after graduation in a Quaker international student work camp and seminar in Japan. There I heard the words *grace* and *agape* for what seemed the first time. I found myself questioning religious people endlessly and questioning whatever came in Quaker silence, seeking the source of the deep stirring in me.

That fall at Harvard I sneaked in several religion courses from Paul Tillich and George Buttrick alongside my Ph.D. program in anthropology, much to the puzzlement of my nonreligious advisor. Other more personal experiences accompanied this, so that by the end of the first term I had finally begun to give birth to an embryonic faith. It was powerful enough an intellectual and emotional conversion to lead me to desert the behavioral sciences as final arbiter of truth, and as vocation as well. I switched to Harvard's Divinity School. Like so many people, I think I confused a call to be a serious Christian with a call to ordination. Hopefully, though, the Spirit at least acquiesced in my desire, since I did move relentlessly in that direction.

After a brief time in the Congregational Church, and a powerful experience in an Episcopal monastery that brought back much of the positive power of my Catholic conditioning, minus its authoritarianism of that time, I became an Episcopalian and a candidate for the priesthood.

3

The Widening Community

The Setting

By 1962 I had finished an extra year of seminary at the Episcopal Theological School in Cambridge (to make me "kosher" for an Episcopal ministry). My old advisor at Harvard, Hans Hofmann, suggested that I begin my ministry in Washington, D.C. "Those people have to pay attention to the world," he said, "they can't escape as easily."

It made sense, though I later found out that Washingtonians can find just about as many ways to escape as any other people. I didn't know much about discernment in those days; I just tried to figure out expediently what seemed best.

After establishing canonical residency in the Episcopal Diocese of Washington, I had a choice of two jobs there. One was to be the assistant at a large established downtown church, with a stable congregation and a rector known for his fine preaching. The other was to be an assistant at what had once been a large neighborhood church that had declined to about two hundred largely

24

vestigial members. The church was in an area of rapid turnover from white to black residents. It had just called a new rector, Bill Wendt, who arrived with a courage, toughness, and commitment to integration bred by his former ministry on the Lower East Side of New York and by a loose band of Anglo-Catholic World War II veterans pledged to a strong social ministry.

I wasn't sure which church was meant for me. The classical church ladder called me to choose the downtown church. That in turn should lead to jobs in "good" churches in the future. To go to a declining inner-city church just beginning to integrate in what was then a rather provincial, pre-civil-rights southern town seemed to promise conflict, tension, poverty, and likely frustration.

Having grown up in the fifties, I knew very little about a social justice ministry firsthand. I had a good theoretical background for it, however, through James Luther Adams and several others at Harvard and a little experience through summers working with social projects of the American Friends Service Committee. And I had tasted the value of organizing the Harvard side of an antinuclear testing demonstration and march to the United Nations (even though I think only ten students from the whole campus responded!).

Felix Kloman, my priest mentor at the time, helped me listen closely to what the Spirit was discerning for me. I sensed that it was meant for me to be in the inner-city church. I had a deep sense of peace about this decision, which I later discovered is a major criterion of Ignatius of Loyola for vocational discernment.

I remember showing up on the steps of the church and walking through its great barnlike interior. I found Bill Wendt's study, and surprised myself with the intensity I felt in wanting to work there. A few weeks later I found

out that the bishop had raised enough money to put me
on the staff there. He hoped that the team ministry Bill
wanted might be able to do something in a place so
precariously yet promisingly situated among different
colors, classes, and values.

Little did he or any of us know then that the church was
to become one of the most famous—or notorious
(depending on your point of view)—of the last several
decades related to civil rights, poverty, liturgy, the peace
movement, and women's ordination: The Church of St.
Stephen and the Incarnation.

I spent the heart of the sixties in that place. Those
years exposed me to more varieties of human interac-
tion, conflict, challenge, tragedy, and beauty than any
comparable period in my life. It taught me my limitations
and squeezed every ounce of imagination, energy, and
faith out of me. All of the basic questions and challenges
of human life seemed to be raised—sometimes all in one
day! Grace seemed to abound in those years, in hard as
well as joyful ways.

Living Together

Home

In June of 1962, freshly ordained, I moved into a room
of the rickety old frame house owned by the church. It sat
alongside the equally old rectory next door to St.
Stephen's. A retired lay couple, Charles and Rosanna
Leete, lived in the house with me. They had decided to
devote much of their remaining active life to a social
ministry that ranged from teaching in a literacy program
to hospitality.

I ate my meals next door in the rectory, where another
single priest, Herbert Aldrich, lived with Bill Wendt
and his family: Mary, his wife, and their three young

children. The Wendts had brought with them from New York an "open rectory" policy, meaning that anyone in need, or wanting to visit, was welcome to come by at any time. The neighborhood had become increasingly poor, and endless cries for help landed at the rectory door, day and night.

Mary Wendt brought a gift of great strength. Never afraid to speak her mind to anyone, seemingly never flagging in energy and ability to cope with every conceivable kind of crisis, full of strong moral concern, she was a stable anchor for all of us in those days.

Bill Wendt was an extremely tough, creative, charming, courageous, visionary, and stubborn urban priest. His religious and social concern derived from his World War II experiences and from his reading and sharing with a group of others the vision and sacrifice of the urban English priests of the nineteenth-century Oxford Movement, which joined radical social concern with a strong sacramental, catholic sense of the church.

Before long we were joined by another priest with the same social concerns, Barry Evans, who moved into my house. Later he brought his new wife Polly. Together we formed an extended family for almost four years.

During the summers we were joined by about seven others—volunteers from Britain, Africa, and around the country—who helped lead a mammoth summer program for the poor neighborhood families. Those years formed my longest and deepest experience in communal living, outside the nuclear family.

A great many experiments in new living arrangements were taking place in the sixties. In Washington alone there were at least fifty recognizable communes. By the end of the decade most had died. The few that survived shared one thing in common: a purpose that tran-

scended end-in-itself community, a purpose defined in
either political or religious terms.

One of my major learnings about communal living
from those days is just that: survival together depends on
having a transcendent purpose, or else your own ego
needs and frustrations related to each other come to
possess and destroy community. The kind of "end-in-
themselves" communities that can survive best, I think,
are monastic communities that are strict about member-
ship and discipline and focus on communal life as a
rooted gift and calling. Family-oriented communities can
and do survive, as well, but the complexities of living and
the sometimes different callings of spouses and children
as they grow up make the survival of such groupings
tenuous.

Another learning about communal living was the great
difference that individual personalities make, especially
in small communities. Our chemistry reacts positively or
negatively to that of others. The positive reactions bring
out one another's light side. The individuals benefit, and
the whole community benefits. The negative reactions
bring out one another's dark side. The individuals
suffer, and the whole community suffers. Experiences of
personal conflict are a kind of purgatory that every
community must expect. They have a way of helping us
bear pain and difference, and realize our limitations in
"making" community happen. All communities live
primarily by grace.

Differences in personality have another consequence.
Introverts need more time in solitude, without having to
feel guilty about not being with everyone all the time.
Solitude rightly lived, after all, is simply a way of being
with everyone in a different way. Physical presence is not
necessary or desirable all the time for authentic
community.

More extroverted people, on the other hand, crave companionship, sharing, conversation, common work. Such people usually have the upper hand in communal living. It is they who most enjoy being together, and who usually press toward a full community vision. Every community is dependent on the drive of such people. They, too, have a right to their way.

Extroverted and introverted people need one another. The former are tempted to escape solitude when they need it. The latter are tempted to escape gatherings when they need them. Therefore living communities need to develop a structure that assures and encourages both. Certain hours of the day can be set aside for common solitude; others can be set aside for mandatory common sharing and work. Without this rhythm, I doubt that any community will long survive.

At St. Stephen's it was our common, overwhelming work that saved us many times. We needed one another's hands, hearts, brains, and prayers constantly. We survived and usually thrived on our differences, as they were brought to bear on ways of carrying out a common ministry. We were not an end-in-itself community by any means. But I think we liked one another, through and despite our differences and tensions.

In any case, we were "given together" at that time; by grace and design we were meant to be together, for the sake of that congregation and neighborhood, for better or worse. That common bond was stronger than anything that came between us. Our gifted times of laughter together helped in that bonding. We were a working commune. Our deepest pleasure was in the fruits of our larger ministry.

In my fifth and last year on the staff at St. Stephen's, much had changed. People had come and gone in our unlabeled commune. The situation no longer made it feasible to eat together. I felt a strong need to be master of my own space. I took an apartment nearby and felt the constant amazement of returning there each day to a predictable sanctuary.

My own self-definition at that time was at the height of ego-centeredness. Never, I think, had I less of a sense of the "co-inherent whole" that I earlier felt, and later rediscovered and deepened. It was a time of self-analysis and exploration in therapy, and with friends. But that was only meant to be a temporary respite. Community came back into focus, but this time in a more limited and intensive sense: with one other human being.

Marriage

I had met Ann Austin as a member of my adult confirmation class several years before. We were drawn together and drew apart and finally were drawn together again, this time for the rest of our lives if God would have it so.

I remember when I crossed the line from ambiguity to the unique love that we can be given for another. I preached an ecstatic sermon that Sunday on love, never mentioning my relation to Ann. But Mary Wendt picked up on the extra "umph" in my words. Right after the service she smiled and said, "Tilden, I think you're in love." Indeed I was, and since authentic love with another is meant to spill over to deeper love for creation and God, it was a very natural and easy sermon.

Eventually with our children Jeremy and Jenny, we formed that way of living together called the nuclear family, extended now and then by our larger blood and human family. There have been times when we have considered joining others in a communal living arrangement, in order to offset the temptations of ecological-economic waste, emotional overintensity, and insulation in the nuclear family, but it just has not been right for us. Personalities and callings are so important in living arrangements. We are not all called to the same way, at the same time.

All of my varied ways of living in community seem to have been right for me at a given time. A nuclear family, on balance, has been right for us at this time. We have an intensive family way of life that seeks to be mutually supportive, God-centered, and caring for the larger world in ways our strengths, callings, sins, and limitations allow. I say this not to hold up the nuclear family as an ideal. I am painfully aware of its limitations and dangers, to which we have succumbed many times. All I am saying is that for us it has been the level of intimate and viable community that we are capable of at this time.

In a small support group a few years ago I remember one married person speaking of her yearning for a larger, mutually covenanted living community. Someone else in the group responded, "I can hardly manage to live with my nuclear family. There's no way I can live intimately with even more people!"

We need to respect one another's experience, scars, and place in community living. At the same time we need to hold up the price and options of every direction, including the price for the larger society. Such knowledge, I hope, can keep us open to other possible, newly called directions for communal living. Perhaps the most important awareness is of the complementarity of different forms of living arrangements, including a sense that no form is meant to be a completely private, end-in-itself means of gratification; all forms are called to be a renewing, refreshing incubator that ultimately bears fruit for the larger community. Ideally, in graced moments, our primary living community will be a microcosm of the larger community where we learn to bear, and be a blessing for, one another.

We all live together in larger units as well: in neighborhoods, organizations, towns, and other levels of common bonding. Our immediate living community is being affected at all these levels, as it is affecting them. On the local level, I remember a sociologist once saying that we never simply buy a house; we buy into a neighborhood and its whole web of relationships, values, and arrangements. Our activity on behalf of the justice, management, and cross-fertilization of this and larger units of living is neglected at our peril.

These can be very frustrating levels to attend to, especially in an atmosphere of growing disillusionment, defensiveness, clashes of values, and sense of helplessness. But, like brushing our teeth, they need to be accepted simply as "givens" that won't go away. We are all called in varying ways and times to those larger dimensions of community.

Summer Heaven

The summers at St. Stephen's brought all layers of community into extraordinary focus and promise. Beginning the summer before I arrived, Bill Wendt continued at St. Stephen's what he had begun at St. Christopher's in New York: a summer program that brought together diverse people to work in and for the neighborhood.

When I arrived at St. Stephen's, I found that I had been put in charge of the summer program, a responsibility, pain, and special joy that was mine throughout my years there. The task, in capsule form, was to bring together the gifts of an enormous range of people on behalf of the neighborhood, whose members in turn would realize and share their own gifts with one another and with those who came.

In hindsight, I know that there was an edge of paternalism involved. The "advantaged" were coming to help the "disadvantaged," even though a number of the staff were also neighborhood people, and all the "advantaged" were clear that they were there to learn as well as to give. Organization of neighborhood people into their own self-determining power block eventually came. But in the early years the initiative rested more with the church's leadership.

It was the early "honeymoon" stage of the sixties' civil rights struggle. Very different people were discovering one another in fresh ways, with a certain mutual vulnerability. It was a particularly personal, and in some ways romantic, phase of the struggle, marked by a frequently common desire to let down the boundaries as much as possible—to find one another—to be reconciled.

Those summer programs provided a frame in which this motive could be lived out—on an international scale. The live-in staff was gathered from many places: "lay volunteers" from Great Britain, black and oriental priests from Nigeria and Singapore, teachers and other workers, college students and seminarians, black, white, oriental, from around the United States. These usually totaled about fifteen people, stuffing the extra rooms of the rectory and the church house next door, and spilling over to the homes of parishioners, except for the few staff who lived in the area.

In this staff core we had specialists in music, drama, arts and crafts, and recreation, and generalists who were group leaders for each of the elementary and junior high age classes that met with us. These leaders developed their own developmental programs for and with the children. The sixties were too young for any clear sense of social-political "conscientization," which today would certainly have been one of the specialties. But some individual staff were farsighted and had their own ways of assisting that process.

We were helped through weekly staff sessions with challenging and visionary social-religious-political leaders of the time. One of the most memorable of these was the presence of a "Little Sister of Jesus," a member of one of those celibate family bands of Roman Catholic Sisters and Brothers inspired by Charles de Foucauld. Each summer one of them would come and show slides of their little communities around the world, always in the poorest places. They live as a witness to Christ in prayer and self-supporting menial work, called to help establish trust in the authenticity of the Christian way by simply incarnating that way among others, refusing any privileges that are not available to the poor workers with whom they live. They adopt local custom and dress whenever possible, even in the style and decoration of their simple chapels.

They believe that Christianity is in disrepute in the world where there is a lack of integrity in its way of life. Thus their small groups seek to embody a simple way of integrity, as a pre-evangelical necessity. They refuse to evangelize. Their work is simply to establish a basis for loving trust, to whittle away at the frequent lack of credibility that is a terrible barrier between Christian and non-Christian, especially among the poor.

This presentation never failed to stir the courage and commitment of the staff—not toward imitation so much as toward a radical vision of the Christian Way, however it is lived.

Each senior group leader in the summer program had a high school assistant. About half of these were middle-class, mostly white teen-agers from outside the neighborhood. The other half were poor or blue-collar neighborhood blacks. For many it was the first, and I fear for some the last, opportunity they'd ever had to develop a regular peer relationship across race and class lines.

There was laughter those summers. Some of the comical relief was at my expense. An especially memorable example of this came in an incident that was a paradigm of the times: our purchase of an old army surplus bus for summer program trips. We had "won" it through a closed-bid auction run by the army. It fell to me to drive with someone to an army base north of Baltimore, an hour and a half away, to get it. We arrived and the person who drove me turned around and headed back to Washington. I was left standing amidst an assortment of very ancient buses that the army had very sensibly retired from active duty.

After signing the necessary forms I was taken to one of the buses, given a key, and waved off. Here I was, clerical collar and all, sitting behind the wheel of an official army bus, with a fast beating heart that knew I had never driven any bus before, and feeling the incongruity of a decidedly civilian priest driving down the highway as though I had just joined the army.

I managed to get the bus started (that was about the only guarantee that went with it), and after testing my capacity to turn the thing around corners, I pulled onto the highway. Once in the inside lane, I figured I would make it to Washington. All I had to do was go straight and slow.

Everything was fine until I got to the middle of the Baltimore Harbor Tunnel, during rush hour. The bus suddenly died. While I sat there desperately trying to get it started, I heard loud sirens go off. The entire tunnel had been closed. Then I saw a tow truck come up to what was now a lonely bus in the middle of a deserted tunnel that was part of the main north-south coastal highway.

The driver wordlessly towed me out, gave my clerical collar and the bus a strange look, and deposited me in the tunnel's parking lot. He then told me that the bus probably had a vapor lock, and sent me to the Tunnel Authority office nearby. Expecting some huge fine, towing fee, and a frowning look of disgust, I was surprised to be given a slip of paper by a grinning official and sent on my way. The paper simply read, "We are sorry that you were inconvenienced!" I could hardly believe it, but not wanting to press my luck I went back to the bus, happy to leave this embarrassing scene.

The bus started again, and I pulled back onto the highway. I hoped the worst was over. But in the middle of nowhere the vapor lock suddenly returned, giving me just enough time to pull onto the shoulder. By this time dusk had fallen. I began to worry that I would be stuck there in the dark without help. I climbed up the bank into the woods to see if there was a house in sight. There wasn't. I went back to the road and stuck out my thumb. Surely someone would think a priest was safe to pick up. The cars whizzed by. The story of the good Samaritan passed through my mind. It was getting dark. A white sports car passed by and then stopped. It backed up. Out of the car stepped a very beautiful young woman. She leaned on the fender, looked at me, and said, "Can I help you?"

It turned out that she was a stripper on her way to work at the Silver Slipper in Washington's porno district. She said that she had once been in love with a man who decided to become a Roman Catholic priest. Out of these fond memories, she had stopped. While driving me for help she told me some of her story. There was a hidden beauty running through it—along with tragedy—a kind of still struggling Mary Magdalene. She told me never to come down to the Silver Slipper. It was just a job for her; she wouldn't justify the place for anyone. She dropped me off at a service station, and I thanked her for the gift she had been for me, in her story as well as her stopping.

The tow truck driver was a Baptist who spent our drive to the bus telling me about his own struggles and actions of faith. Since I now had help, the bus, contrary to the end, started immediately. This time I made it all the way home.

As we were transforming the bus's drab army green into a bright civilian blue I reflected on how much had come together in that little episode: contributions from all kinds of people that allowed us to buy the bus, military personnel, tunnel authorities, a stripper becoming a good Samaritan, a blue-collar Baptist sharing his heart. As a result we had a badly needed vehicle that would take neighborhood people, along with a near cross section of the rest of the world, to beaches (some had never seen the ocean), museums, parks, plays, and demonstrations. That was the way grace seemed to happen then: drawing people and institutions together, unintentionally and intentionally, in a way that served God's vision of co-inherence.

This vision was manifest in many other ways during the summer, especially in chapel. Each day began in the big nave of the church. At the height of these programs, this meant about two hundred children and eighty staff people. Our diversity was immense, yet there we were, trying to see our common rootedness in one compassionate, reconciling Source of Life. We dealt with everything imaginable during those half hours, and in every imaginable way: our relation to God, our social vision, personal morality and prayer, which were conveyed through drama, music, movement, scripture, story, and any other way the staff could think of.

I think these were very important periods, ones that later were lost as government-funded programs came to the fore with their normal abhorence and incomprehension of anything other than safe, secular, technical program content. Without this deeper religious focus together, it is so much easier to give in to the temptations of narrow individual and group power interests that lose a fuller vision and awareness of who we are as human beings and what we're here for. Without that level of challenge and struggle, little idols and big egos abound (these are rampant enough even with attention to that level)!

Every Friday night the live-in-staff was invited over to someone's house for dinner. Usually these hosts and hostesses were searching liberals anxious to find connection with that larger human world from which the "arrangements" of American society had cut them off. Sometimes it was the first time a black or oriental person had ever crossed their door (at least in a social capacity), and the first time such persons had crossed into whole neighborhoods on this basis. They became witnesses to inclusion that were not always well received by neighbors. For some of those families it helped lead to gradually deeper involvement and commitment in struggles for human justice.

I remember one of those evenings that was spent with Gerry Lanigan. She was a tall, stately, beautiful woman whose magnificent singing voice beguiled anyone privileged to hear her. She had lit countless candles that evening, turning the house into a flickering wonderland. After dinner Bill Wendt spoke for all, "Sing for us, Gerry!" We gathered around her piano where we sat speechless, except to occasionally suggest songs and arias, as she sang to us of love, sorrow, beauty, nature, God, and community.

Such an evening always brings out the vivid power of authentic song to embody, yet always transcend, nitty-gritty human realities. Song brings out of us a perspective, a dignity, an acceptance of mystery and paradox, and a strange, shared strength. No wonder heaven is always portrayed by music rather than dialogue!

The grand finale each summer was a gigantic festival that took weeks of preparation and everyone's involvement. A neighborhood cleanup and rat hunt was organized. Special recognition was given the person who killed the largest rat. Rats proliferated in alley garbage and became a menace to health. (Rat bites, particularly to babies, were not uncommon.)

Parents and other neighborhood adults whom staff had met through visits and special programs were asked to use their personal skills to help the children and staff with the festival. Together we made booths, costumes, floats, banners, contests, food, music, and much more.

The great day began in church with a festive Eucharist that pulled out all the stops: incense, chant, song, endless vestments, flowers, banners, ecumenical concelebrants at the altar. The church usually was packed with about seven hundred people from all around the metropolis, a marvelous assortment of humanity finding common cause together.

Then the Eucharist spilled into the streets with a great singing procession into which everyone willing was gathered, led usually by a bishop, who was as often African as American.

It was followed by a day-long carnival that filled the church parking lot, yards, and the church itself. Everyone came.

I can remember the moment when it all came together for me one summer. The festival day was half over. I knew the suffering and joy, the gifts and scars of so many of them. There were others about whose lives I could only guess.

At that instant I sensed the deep "all rightness" of everything that was happening. Someone was moving through all of this, affirming not so much our particular efforts, but ourselves as we were—in and beyond our actions. I breathed a great sigh of relief. Indeed, the Holy One was intimately present and moving through all that was happening. For the moment, I could appreciate this realization with a soft smile.

That was a little taste of "sabbath" time, which was to become much more integrated in my life later. It felt simply like a yielding to grace in our midst, a proper ending to a "summer heaven," a little sign of God's hope for us.

Heaven is spotty to our vision and experience, though. The summer passed; the tragedy and complicity of human barriers continued to reveal themselves.

4

Color and Culture: Barriers and Gifts

I remember running into two little black sisters, who were crying, in front of the church hall one afternoon. Inside a film about contemporary Africa was being shown as part of our after-school enrichment program. When I asked them why they were crying, they blurted out that their mother had told them that Africans were savages. They didn't have to say any more. It quickly dawned on me that they knew those Africans were their distant relatives, and they were ashamed. I remember how many years I had had it drummed into my head when I was studying anthropology that there was no such thing as a "primitive" people. There were only literate and nonliterate cultures. The latter could be far more sophisticated than the former in all but technological know-how.

But not many people were exposed to anthropology in those days. Certainly not those little girls or their parents. They were exposed instead to the still-prevalent American assumption that white, usually Western European, is the height of culture and superiority, and that it was incumbent on every real American to assimilate as much

as possible of its fine clothing. What you can't appropriate for yourself (like color, if you're not white), you must
accept as just tough luck.

Theologically, of course, this was nonsense as much as
it was anthropologically, but theology often was in the
head, learned in a segregated milieu; the heart was in the
culture, and had its way of appearing even in the best
"liberal."

My own physical appearance put me in an unusual
position. Despite my mongrel European background,
the Mediterranean features clearly won out, with some
exaggeration that confused people: kinky dark hair, fat
lips, high cheek bones, brown eyes, swarthy complexion.
For years I heard stories of blacks asking others what I
really was: black? Hispanic? white? Of course, racial
mixtures didn't mean much in the American caste
system. You were one thing or the other. It didn't really
count to be both (though within the black community it
can make a difference).

I have always felt it providential that I could "pass" in
so many directions. I sometimes kept quiet about what I
really was, so that as many people as possible might let me
bridge to them. But I couldn't hide from myself the fact
that I indeed was white in experience, and that I could
only share vicariously the suffering of another race in
America. I must be accountable with the white majority
for its ways of "arranging" things to be stacked against
anyone of "color." At least I could claim a real mixture in
terms of ethnic background. More and more I came to
identify with the more oppressed cultures from which I
sprang, culminating in that trip to Wales in the summer
of 1980.

Those five years at St. Stephen's brought me into
intimate contact with almost every nuance of race and
culture (including class) that I could ever hope to

experience in so short a time. I saw many gifts and weaknesses offered the human family through these differences. But I also became very clear that these differences are real and easily become insurmountable barriers and points of alienation without a powerfully transcendent commitment to a vision of pluralism in God.

The motto of the Episcopal Society for Cultural and Racial Unity in those days was taken from Psalm 133: "Behold, how good and joyful a thing it is for brethren to dwell together in unity" (women in those days still comfortably fitting under "brethren"). That was our vision then. Integration was the password. Of course, integration was strongly one way: *into* mainline white culture, at least bordering on assimilation. Black differences at first weren't very respected.

Then Stokely Carmichael preached at St. Stephen's. That controversial and electrifying moment symbolized the beginning change from white initiative and power toward black. It was a wrenching time as everyone struggled to try out new ways of relating, and separating. St. Stephen's became a center of every variety of civil rights activity and conflict of visions. The movement was lived out in microcosm there, as in so many other places.

Being in the heart of the nation's capital, there was the added burden and privilege of being the organizing and sleeping ground for all kinds of groups who came to Washington to place their grievances before the powers that be. The culminating moment of those nationally focused gatherings was the great March on Washington to the Lincoln Memorial on that hot August day of 1963. The summer program was in session. We helped organize a march from the church for everyone who wanted to join us in the neighborhood. We wanted to make it as much a witness of the church as possible, so we decided to walk behind a processional cross and several gospel-related banners.

Just before setting out I walked through the nave of the church and ran into Moses Oyenladi, a Nigerian Anglican priest who was working in the program with us that summer. He had been adamant about staying behind, feeling that what we were doing was an American affair in which a foreign national shouldn't get involved. Now he was looking very excited and rushed toward the door to join us. He said that he had just been strongly moved by the Spirit to come—that it was his battle, too.

A motley crowd of hundreds marched for miles down Sixteenth Street toward the Lincoln Memorial. On the way we were joined by thousands of others organized by other churches.

On the steps of St. John's Church, across from the White House at the bottom of Sixteenth Street, we paused to lead a litany of prayer for the day. Then we were lost in the waves of people coming from all directions as we continued toward the feet of Martin Luther King and his dream—our dream.

That dream continued through the Poor People's Campaign, shifted from race to a focus on poverty. The goal (at least in popular vision) dwelt on the "haves" allowing more room for the "have-nots" of color and poverty without the haves really giving up anything, except a little imperialism. Everyone was to be brought up to the standards of white middle-class rights and wealth, and hopefully more shared community. It was an expansive time with an expansive dream. There's room for everyone at the top (or at least in the middle), with just the right rearrangements.

The first great crack in the dream was revealed to me very personally through the hard empirical research of

Dr. Ivor Kraft. Ivor, a research social scientist at HEW, approached me one year and asked if he could interview the black and white teen-agers working in the summer program and observe their interactions. After gaining our consent, he became a silent shadow always lurking near in meetings and activities during the summer. He was a farsighted researcher, sensing that we were in a phase of unusual openness across racial, ethnic, and class lines, and that it would not last likely more than five years. He wanted to learn as much as possible about how very different groups of human beings moved together and apart during such a period.

Ivor followed up on the life trajectories of the poor or blue-collar black teen-agers and the upper-middle-class white teen-agers working in the program. What happened to them a year after their fine summer together? The results were devastating.

Most of the whites were doing well in school and finding themselves positioned by motivation and opportunity to go on to the best colleges and career tracks. Many of the blacks, on the other hand, were already beginning to fall off the "ladder": into crime, family trouble, disillusionment, and crippling poverty. Thus in just one year, the trajectories of these two different class and racial groups had begun to diverge dramatically farther. There were exceptions, but indeed they were just that: exceptions.

This awareness was deepened by my experience with the poor rural whites settled in one section of our parish. I watched so many of their children slowly become eaten alive by a whole constellation of destructive forces. With some of these forces the people were accomplices. Sin is real with poor people as with others. But with many they simply seemed victims.

I still carry some guilt about refusing confirmation to

Linda. She came with a veil, all excited about the rite. But she never would come to confirmation class. It didn't seem fair to the others or to her own dignity to let the rite be so cheap. So it seemed at the time. Now I realize a little better at what cost her whole life was lived. She had come to present herself for what she must vaguely have sensed as a rite of her affirming dignity in God and the community. Today I would ask her just such a question about its meaning to her and let her be presented if there was any positive awareness of God in her life at all. As it was, law won over gospel in my denseness. She was crestfallen, and never returned.

It became devastatingly clear to me that patterns of race and class were deeply imbedded in the whole way life was arranged in America. So much was just inexorably stacked against such teen-agers in what came to be called "the system." Even in this most open of times, the opening was but a tiny crack compared to what dramatic rearrangements, energy, and time it would take to really help things come out differently for more than the most gifted and fortunate few.

That realization has not changed with time. Indeed, it has been deepened as we have moved from a time of expansion to one of scarcity. Even then I was beginning to realize that there simply were not enough resources under current technological and social conditions to allow everyone to be in the middle, much less at the top. The first romantic and relatively easy stage of justice had been largely successful. It did not require a radical new life style for any of the "haves." With scarcity, however, the goal of justice becomes reversed: not to get everyone moved up, but for everyone to begin looking at how they might voluntarily move down toward greater sharing of power and goods. That was one of the hard sayings of Jesus that only monastics and a few sects managed to institutionalize well historically, and even they have had trouble sticking with it whenever much wealth was around.

The rise to visibility of the Third and Fourth Worlds simply reinforced this awareness that we were involved in a much more difficult situation than many of us had thought. People may at their best be willing to share power and goods, but not to reduce the amount they have. That is a graced act of the highest order when it is voluntary, especially when they are bombarded in school and commercial media and often at home day by day about how important it is to have so much.

It seemed that nothing, short of an ever-deeper conversion into a way of life geared to values not dependent on material or power possessions as ultimate, could avoid raging conflict and delusion in the future.

The inadequacy of the secularized "collective" values that forcibly tried to replace these private ones in most socialist countries is apparent in the craving for those private goods and powers that seem ever to gather momentum among those peoples. Conversion must be deeper than this, indeed, it must go to the very core of how people see their purpose in life, and to the graced nature of a human being. Authentic Christian faith has much to offer this conversion. This view has remained a constant with me through all these years.

Christian faith includes a realism about human nature along with its vision. I have no delusions about any humanly constructable utopia. Accumulation and misuse of power and goods are an intrinsic potential of our paranoid, confused, sinful nature. But so is the image of God that we are through and beneath that nature. I have enduring hope in God through our brokenness, and constant wonder at our demonstrated capacity for divine cooperation. Yet any social-political vision must account for both dimensions of our nature, lest it lead us to oppression or despair. A rhythm of visionary sabbath time with functional ministry time in our lives, which I will elaborate later, can be vital in fostering a way of life that accounts for our full human nature and hope. Liturgy, to which I will now turn, is one dimension of visionary sabbath time.

5

Liturgy and Cooperation

The Ordering Center

At its best liturgy presents authentic Christian faith, again and again and again. Support and empowerment for ever-deeper conversion into the heart of God and creation is found around that holy table, and that loaf and fruit of the vine, and in that Word ever breaking open our narrow minds. It is in common worship that Christians are most uniquely present to one another.

Bill Wendt brought to St. Stephen's his strong Anglo-Catholic sacramentalism. We shared with other clergy responsibility for daily Eucharist as well as Morning and Evening Prayer, and monthly communions for the many shut-ins of the parish. The liturgical calendar, including saints days, was followed scrupulously, especially in the early years.

I came to value deeply the ordering of life these services gave to the day and week. I had come to the parish after many years in a very ordered academic world. It didn't take long to realize how much real, everyday life in a crowded, wildly heterogeneous neighborhood was lived on the edge of chaos. The wide-openness of the parish's future direction at the time, encouraging every conceivable kind of experiment, added to a sense of living on that edge myself. I was brought to tears more than once in realizing my own limitations of energy and compassion in the midst of daily schedules that gyrated between hospitals, shut-ins, alcoholics, near suicides, hustlers, suburban people wanting to help and understand, teen-agers wanting to destroy and create simultaneously, church and neighborhood groups and programs needing planning, teaching, sharing, and pastoring.

It was to the altar that my frequently helpless sense was brought, and my true center was sought. Sometimes I was so tired and saturated by so much going on in and around me that I just went through the motions of words and movements with a dull, listless mind. Was it all real, this Christ, this Eucharist, this Book, this God? Is anybody really there? Why don't I see more transformation in and around me?

Sometimes it just felt a sham, and me a false shaman. But fidelity was very important in high Anglican tradition (to the point sometimes of utter sterility!). For me the regularity of those services was the anchor, and often the sail, in my life.

Before coming to St. Stephen's I was privileged to spend the summer on a study tour of the liturgical reform movement in Europe. Bill Wendt, counter to the liturgical rigidity so frequent in Anglo-Catholic tradition (and in those days in Evangelical Episcopal tradition as well), was very open to anything that would help present the fullness of the gospel to the people. He was a key member of the Associated Parishes, a national organization trying to instill liturgical reform in parishes regardless of church-manship. Little by little much was changed.

Taking our cue from the Left Bank Parisian community of St. Severin, the Taizé ecumenical community, and other centers of renewal, we introduced four innovations on Sundays. First was the kiss (or sign) of peace, an early practice of the church before Communion, dramatizing the Lord's words about being reconciled with your brother/sister before partaking. It remained only vestigially in Catholic Solemn Eucharists where the priest, deacon, and subdeacon exchanged a kind of pro forma, distant, ceremonial "hug." It no longer belonged to the people at all.

A little historical research revealed to me that it had disappeared in the late Middle Ages after people had begun to fight over the status of who got it first! It seemed a most vital act to restore, especially in a place like St. Stephen's, which was so intent upon justly reconciling divided peoples. We introduced it in the form used in the ecumenical Church of South India: one person putting his palms over the closed palms of a neighbor, who in turn passes it on.

This proved a powerful restoration of a lost liturgical gem. For the first time people had to touch their neighbor—not a very common thing in staid Episcopal tradition at the time. This could be traumatic. I will never forget watching a rather hostile, self-enclosed older white lady try to rub off the touch of her black neighbor after she had been passed the peace.

That incident reminded me of a penetrating remark of Massey Shepherd, a liturgical scholar, who warned that liturgical reform would serve only to place a flashlight beam on the emptiness of a congregation if its inner life is not transformed with it. That transformation is not in our hands. But we can symbolize how it is meant to look—in little gestures like the peace. Indeed, perhaps we will find the peace to be much more than a gesture, since touch is the primary means of imparting the Spirit in Scripture.

Now I am glad to say that the passing of the peace has become common and formally sanctioned in many churches, especially in Episcopal and Roman Catholic ones. It has always been present informally outside the liturgy in the handshake encouraged in many Protestant churches at the end of the service. I do not think, though, that this can carry the full power and symbolism of the reconciling peace given the neighbor at the very heart of the liturgy.

The second innovation was a food basket placed in the center aisle, into which people were encouraged to bring canned food and dry goods as material offerings for our neighborhood food bank. It frequently was filled and brought to the altar with the rest of the congregation's weekly offerings. Again, such a practice is more widespread today, in one form or another.

The third change involved music. Chanting was part of the parish's liturgical tradition, along with traditional hymns. There was something missing, though, between those old hymns and plainsong chanting. We filled this hole, at least for a while, with the gentle, lyrical Gelineau Psalms from France, which included a special, easy, repetitive antiphon that the congregation could sing antiphonally with the cantor. Later, with the help of Barry Evans, who came aboard the staff with a liturgical specialization, we added many kinds of contemporary religious folk music, including more and more black spirituals.

Mother Scott, a wise old black woman from Mississippi, added a quantum leap to our black repertoire when she joined the congregation. During the years after I left St. Stephen's, she grew in public stature as she sang and commercially recorded songs of love, pain, faith, and struggle from the South, some of her own composition. She brought us all together many times in many ways. Her death a few years ago brought a huge cross section of Washington folk to her funeral service, witnessing to the ways she and her music had been an instrument of the Spirit among us.

The final innovation had to do with the clothing of ministers and the use of space. Simplicity was a clarion call of the liturgical reform movement. Vestments and altar coverings needed to be generously full, of simple material, and simple yet bold in design. It was time to give a decent burial to the fancy lace, heavy gold brocades, uninspired mass-produced crosses, and ostentatious, complicating trappings. This was a time for rediscovering the simple, creative, obscure heart of the faith, represented not by magisterial priests, but by servant ministers, sharing the ministry of the whole congregation.

Space was needed to reflect these concerns, as well. The triumphal, hard stone altar against the wall was replaced by a simple yet dramatic table, behind which the presiding celebrant could face the people. A fenceless raised circle surrounded the table, around which people could stand and receive the sacrament together. Font and pulpit surrounded this center.

Later the front pews were removed, so children and others who wanted to could sit in a more open place. My dream has always been to have *all* the pews removed (except for a few around the walls for older people), and leave everyone in a huge, hopefully rugged, open space, as in Russian Orthodox and Muslim tradition, and now in the ecumenical Taizé Community as well. But we had already gone as far as we dared go, and it was a dramatic change. The environment now was warm, inviting, uncluttered, simply focused. We could worship together with the space helping us rather than impeding us.

Such a space, after all, is meant to be an embodiment of the gospel. It is more than incidental, even though the Holy Spirit is able to break through the most uninviting space. But why put roadblocks in the way? Why not prepare the Way of the Lord for people in the environment that clothes them in church?

I remember preaching one Sunday about the building as a bloody cross. The nave and large attached parish hall were in constant use and abuse in those days (and still today): day-care centers, community organizations, children's programs daily (breakfast, after school, summer), drama, choirs, religion classes, church guilds, civil rights rallies, teen-age dances, fights, rapes, robberies, alcoholics throwing up in the bathrooms, lineups of the poor every day for counsel, food, and money, the regular meetings of the "Loser's Club" of older neighborhood status-less, in-trouble people (later becoming the "Winner's Club"!). An endless stream of humanity left the building torn and bloodied, as indeed it was called to be. How much more important this made the sanctuary; we all needed a place of simple, ordered beauty where we could be strengthened and quieted. I remember one seven-year-old girl telling her mother that she liked to go to church here because it was "clean." What she meant, her mother said, is that it was quiet and simple—a true sanctuary amidst a noisy, turbulent world. That was and is a basic offering of the church for everyone.

But prayer liturgies can take place more directly in that noisy, turbulent world. The occasion I remember best was during a demonstration for the integration of an amusement park outside Baltimore. An integrated group of about ten of us from St. Stephen's were there. During a period when everyone was milling around in the park late in the afternoon, we gathered in a circle and began to read Evening Prayer together from *The Book of Common Prayer*. People gathered around us and participated in the prayers that were familiar to them. The staid old words, so often repeated by my lips, came alive in a totally fresh way. Confession and absolution of sins, petitions, intercessions, thanksgivings, praise, scripture, canticles—all of these incarnated themselves in this moment of risk, witness, and hope. I became aware of the authenticity of the words in this very real situation of testing. They were meant to be prayed there.

A little of that prayer anonymously made it into the evening TV news. I was very glad for that. Somehow it gave the full perspective and depth of motivation for Christians in such a demonstration—perspective and depth needed to offset the heated, narrowing polarizations that are so tempting at such times for participants and viewers alike.

That kind of incarnate prayer was very natural for most evangelical black Christians in such situations. Even in the discussion and planning of demonstrations and neighborhood social action, when such black Christians were in charge, the words spoken to one another wove together prayer, scripture, discussion, and action like the strands of the single rope of life that they are. Liberal white Christians often had more trouble with this integration, tending more to separate prayer and action (or to collapse prayer completely into action). Black Christians taught everyone else much about an incarnate corporate faith and prayer in those days. This integration is seen later in such places as the Chicano Farm Workers' struggle led by César Chávez, and in the Masses celebrated on the Pentagon steps, based on earlier civil rights precedents.

St. Stephen's extended its liturgical life into the community, especially during Holy Week. On Palm

Sunday the whole congregation processed around the neighborhood at the start of the main service, singing and passing our palms to many amazed people on the streets.

Lest this sign of hope seem too unreal in such a very poor neighborhood, it was followed on Good Friday with another procession through the neighborhood that was much more existentially understood. This one included a large cross. We stopped at a number of "stations" that seemed very fitting on Good Friday: places where people had been evicted from their homes, drugged, raped, or suffered in some other way during the past year. At each station prayers were offered, and the cross visibly enfolded the pain. Parishioners returned for a simple rice and beans supper and contributions for and talk about places of suffering, in the light of the cross.

Such a procession and reflection together, augmented by altars and tabernacles stripped of all signs of life, aided our awareness of the darkness shared by the world outside of God's Providence. We felt that sadness as we huddled together in darkness shortly before midnight on Holy Saturday, a microcosm of the world, waiting for a sign of the Saving One promised us.

In such a community, the new fire of Easter kindled amidst the darkness was more than a liturgical charade. It was that which finally allowed survival and hope amidst struggle and despair. It came not apart from the darkness, but out of its midst, and was passed, person to person, candle to candle, until everyone shared the light meant for all. Those candles gave only a flickering, shadowy light that did not end the darkness, yet they seemed enough for us now to be and see and do what was needed, while praying ceaselessly for the fullness of God's reign when all will be light.

The bells of the resurrection rang, and we gathered as one body into the eternal procession of celebration.

Working Together

Our life at St. Stephen's was centrally ordered by liturgy, but around that it was run by a team ministry. Bill Wendt was very committed to such a model for the parish's leadership. This meant that all clergy functions were shared as equally as possible: preaching, celebrating, hearing confessions, serving communions to shut-ins, even attending vestry meetings. This showed an enormous amount of trust in a neophyte like me and others on the team. I was honored by Bill's attitude; it energized me to do the very best job I could.

Team ministries, to be effective, require both rapport and much meeting together. Despite the differences of the various priests and lay workers who were part of the staff during those years, we usually did share commitment to an open, imaginative liturgy and a socially concerned parish. We also usually liked one another, which is always a grace in itself.

Every Saturday morning we met together for several hours. Part of the meeting was nuts and bolts about who was doing what, when. But some kind of informal creative envisioning time always managed to be included, planned, or otherwise. That kind of time was greatly expanded during the overnight staff retreats that we took together every few months.

Bill loved creative ferment. I think he even enjoyed the crises. At least he really came alive in them—and there were plenty of opportunities. I, on the other hand, enjoyed a certain modicum of predictable life and activity (though I loved imaginative approaches to these). Not accidentally, this led me to be the primary staff person responsible for education: an arena that requires a certain planned stability. I taught both youth and adult confirmation classes and organized the church school

and after-school programs with much lay assistance. I
also helped organize an adult forum that came to take the
place of the traditional coffee hour. People sat down with
their coffee around tables and listened to some religious
or community speaker; discussed among themselves
their own concerns, responses, and needs; made
contributions in response to pleas for various causes; as
well as just enjoyed one another. After the main service
most people came to these.

Each forum became a test of how much difference and
challenge people could bear. The climate of the times
fostered far more stretching of boundaries together than
would have seemed imaginable a few years before. Most
of us in the parish shared a strong sense of common
purpose; people from all over the metropolis, as well as
from the neighborhood, were joining and volunteering
for service. Class, though, remained a barrier that could
be crossed by just so many, and for so long. Some black
and white families left because of our attempts to include
more blue-collar and especially more really poor,
status-less people. Others joined for this very reason. It
was a most experimental time. How far could we go with
one another across various lines and form a really
comprehensive team ministry? How much could the
church really contribute to the spiritual and social lives of
parishioners, neighbors, city?

For everyone it was both exhilarating and exhausting.
I remember one leading layman saying that he needed a
month off from the church about every three months,
because he just couldn't take the constant newness,
disorientation, and demands that were standard each
week. There was a multiplier effect to whatever we did
that was new: new criticism and praise was produced,
new work borne, new people and meetings to contend

with, and heaven knows what unpredictable other results. The worst side of this was that sometimes we fell into the trap of doing something new because it was expected, both by staff and by many others. We could not let ourselves trust anything stabilizing—except the liturgy, and even that constantly had new clothes.

In hindsight, though, I think we were called to be unrelentingly experimental in those years. The church was positioned in such a way that it had freedom to try what other churches could not, without paying a much higher price. Our experiment was not for St. Stephen's alone. It was for the whole church. That is why so much publicity came our way. It wasn't for St. Stephen's as such; it was to communicate that which was possible for others—not always *right* for others (or even for St. Stephen's in the long run), but what was *possible*.

I remember Parker Palmer, a friend and urban sociologist, saying once that what people most needed was a sense of alternative possibilities. Ironically, the more specialized and highly educated you are, he said, the *less* sense of possibility you often feel: only a very few jobs and places fit what a Ph.D. is educated for. But the possibilities for the person who happens to have a Ph.D. in fact are much broader than he or she usually thinks, just as they are for others. St. Stephen's opened wide the door of possibilities for all sorts and conditions of people: possibilities for relationships, liturgy, social involvement, education, work style, living arrangements, creative conflict, creative cooperation.

Peace

The sense of alternatives escalated to international scale when the Vietnam War developed. It seemed a big step from race, class, and poverty to international conflict. But as so many came to realize, it really was the same struggle, projected globally.

I remember my first sermon against the war, before there was broadscale public demonstration against it. At the time I would have been thrown out of most parishes for it, especially in an area with so many military personnel. Even at St. Stephen's in that early time it was a step that was controversial. At the parish forum afterward, a woman whose husband was a marine colonel in Vietnam publicly excoriated me for focusing on the poor peasants in Vietnam rather than on the danger to our troops there. She was right. I had been too one-sided. Even with massive armaments, our troops did suffer dramatically—and not only the troops, but also their families and the divided conscience of the whole nation.

But the Vietnamese, Communist and non-Communist, suffered much more dramatically. In the midst of a war it is very difficult to remember the other side. War by its very nature cuts a gaping chasm between our once united humanity. The gospel forbids us ever to see that chasm as ultimate, or as an excuse to deny the equal humanity of those temporarily cut away from us. Without this awareness there is nothing but uncertain expediency left to restrain the full power of human capacity for endless destruction.

St. Stephen's was a center of the antiwar movement, especially in the height of it which was after I left the staff. It was inevitable. There is no way we could cut off all our learnings about poverty and race and our vision for a just community when looking at the relations of nation-states.

For me, though, it was never a clean picture. I knew that America was playing its old imperial game in Southeast Asia. At the same time, so were the Communists. Their seriousness about social justice seemed greater than ours; Vietnam needed that justice. But they did not seem serious about or understand full *human* justice and vision as I have received these in Christian tradition. Substituting an aggrandizing collective ego in totalitarian state socialism for the aggrandizing private ego prevalent in today's capitalism indeed may provide fuller social justice. But if this is imposed with no sense of a transcendent definition and purpose for humanity, and no respect for the partial mystery of pluralistic human callings that the state cannot determine, then we have exchanged one inadequately human system for another. The severe persecution by the triumphant Communist Vietnamese of active Buddhists, Christians, and, after the war, others who had any vision beside or beyond their own confirmed my suspicions. Even their seeming capacity for social justice later appeared to break down as old ethnic and new Communist imperialistic instincts took over in Laos and Cambodia.

I do not claim to have all the facts in asserting these opinions. When do we ever have all the facts? I must remain open to new insight. But these were my feelings about that agonizing war. They still mark my international political attitude.

Recently I read a number of little stories by American soldiers about the Vietnam War. It brought back to me the horror of that war, and of any war.

I share the frustrations of many today who see the utter insanity of over half a trillion dollars of the world's limited resources going toward military budgets, which among other lethal weapons have amassed the equivalent of 1.3 million Hiroshima bombs. We simply cannot survive and thrive together on this small, utterly interdependent planet with the attitudes we have inherited—attitudes of *ultimate* loyalty to narrowly defined self-interests of the nation-state or of its

sometime-substitutes in the world today: the multina-
tional corporation or international Communism and
other power blocks. True patriotism involves loyalty to
whatever will help the people live with one another in
peace, freedom, and justice and will help the ecology of
one's homeland. Such a homeland today must be
stretched to see that it touches and ultimately includes all
the land of this tiny, integral earth, even if our special
responsibility is for one part of it.

This is a declaration (certainly not the first) of the real
patriotism to which we are called today. It is not a
devaluation of valid national patriotism. Indeed, after
the return of the American Iranian hostages I had a
classically patriotic dream. In it, I was driving down a city
street and was overwhelmed to the point of tears with a
deep, loving sense of the nurture given me in so many
ways by this land and its people, despite its countless
shortcomings.

The fulfilment of that patriotic love now, though, must
see how surely we as a nation have become a neighborhood of one world city, where what happens anywhere
eventually will affect us, or our children. Christian
concern is not simply for security in this situation, but for
whatever aids our movement toward a just, pluralistic,
mutually respectful and mutually correcting planetary
society. Only when that is approximated can we hope for
any modicum of real security and peace.

I was heartened and amazed to learn recently of an
incipient "earth battalion" in the U.S. Army, organized
by a few visionary officers. In one of its publications
Colonel James Channon summarizes its work:

> The First Earth Battalion is a growing network of warriors
> with the planet in mind. Their business is the ethical evolution
> of force. They seek mastery as they move consistently up the

ethical hierarchy of force: from Force of Arms, to Force of Will; to Force of Spirit; and finally to Force of Heart. Recent world events clearly show that alternative forms of force are needed and that the good in people needs more expression in the arenas of power and conflict.

The battalion is evolving lessons in moral combat from the New Age forces presently collecting on the social frontiers throughout the world. . . . We find that New Age Samurai are sprinkled throughout the world just waiting for a common banner under which they can serve . . . rooted in service to people, planet, and the many paths to God.[1]

The proposed missions of such a "battalion" are manifold, ranging from rescue companies in national, ecological, and human disasters, to pioneers in urban, ecological, and space settings, to counterforce groups between armies on the brink of fighting. It would also include training of others in such "soft tactics" as ethical combat, universe awareness, loving teamwork, and the integration of mind, body, and spirit.

It is interesting that the First Earth Battalion has chosen a version of the "warrior monk" as its model, focused on the development of conscience and spiritual awareness along with the ability to neutralize an attacker. When I read this I was reminded of an informal day I spent about eight years ago with a group of military officers and church personnel at the Pentagon. We shared common job descriptions in our respective arenas: assistance with constructive and needed organizational change. In the process of comparing notes we were all surprised to find some of the overlaps in historical military and church motivation: both felt called to "save" the society in some way; both harked back to a

[1]*The First Earth Battalion,* available from James Channon, 11000 Wilshire Blvd., Suite 10104, Los Angeles, CA. 90024.

"covenant" (Scripture and the Constitution), and both valued discipline, as well as obedience to a higher force than personal ego. God could be dangerously identified with narrow national interests on both sides, but God could be seen to transcend these interests as well.

I was not prepared to find so many parallels. But that day helped prepare me to understand how such a concept as the First Earth Battalion could emerge.

Perhaps this points to the possibility that out of the very heart of the military world, so despairing and frightening to so many people, we may find important leadership that will help empower a shift in the nature and function of our armed forces and the vision of nation-states in the years ahead. This would be a radically different kind of leadership than we see in nations taken over by military juntas whose motivation is a repressive attempt to freeze a society in the name of order and security.

I am well aware of the immense difficulties in accomplishing such a shift, in the light of history, national differences, aggression, fears, and myopically defined self-interests. But it is toward the imagination for such a shift that energy must be steadily and courageously directed in the years ahead, not just by dissidents outside the controlling structures of power, but perhaps especially by those who carry that power in our name. The alternative ultimately is collective suicide or barbarism: a betrayal of our stewardship of God's earth. Current armaments holding one another at bay can at best be a limited, extremely risky, and costly holding action until such bold imagination is forthcoming and broadly acted upon.

6

Pastors and an Upset World

Shaping the Urban Priest/Minister

Many seminarians worked with us in my years at St. Stephen's. Seminaries on the whole were not equipped to provide adequate preparation for socially active clergy in those days. There was nothing between the disorienting field experience that many seminarians were having and their often unbridged academic classes. Bill Wendt, myself, and a few others looked at what we could do about this. The upshot was the Washington Urban Training Program, approved eventually by two Protestant and three Roman Catholic theological schools in the area, with myself as part-time director.

This was my first step away from St. Stephen's, even though it involved only a day a week of my time. It gave room for my experiential educational instincts to expand. I threw myself into its organization with a passion. The seminarians were allowed twelve hours a week for a combination of field placements and seminars. I arranged placements in every conceivable type of setting, from local grassroots community

organizations to bureaucracies. The interdependence of
the whole metropolitan area grew in our consciousness to
the point that we came to see the foolishness of looking
for positive, enduring change in the city without
complementary action in the suburbs. It was one
interdependent whole in many ways.

The seminars were wildly speculative and visionary,
pushing and testing every possibility for human social
arrangements and theological justification. The primary
seminar leaders included three people: Richard Kauff-
man, a researcher for the Joint Economic Committee of
Congress, a very sane young lawyer, full of integrity and
steadiness; Milton Kotler, a political scientist and strong
theoretician for more extensive local community government; and Robb Burlage, a brilliant, inspiring young
economist full of social moral vision. The last two were
faculty of the Institute for Policy Studies, a kind of "rad
lib" think tank, in whose always bustling offices we met.
Two Jews and a nonpracticing Christian: the kind of
differences that didn't matter much in those days;
indeed they enhanced seminarian interest as long as the
people involved had prophetic blood and clear heads.

Robb in particular had an edge of holiness that he
certainly would never admit. He cared for human
suffering, justice, and full human vision with heart,
mind, and soul. His brilliance saw the holes in all varieties
of social schemes, yet without the sarcastic cynicism that
so easily comes to those who see through everything.
Beyond his iconoclasm was an indestructible hope that to
me was graced, even if he would have a hard time naming
the Giver. He was one of those secret friends of God
through whom we are inspired to continually move
through and beyond all idols, never giving up hope in
high human purpose.

One little episode was very characteristic. He decided

that he would no longer let someone at the office do his typing. He would do his own typing. He didn't make a big deal out of this. He simply did it. In his mind, that was part of the integrity of full social justice in his situation.

The Roman Catholic seminarians were all members of religious communities. On the whole, they contrasted markedly with the Protestants. The latter tended to be very individualistic, unformed in any consistent theological position, and creative. The Catholics were more disciplined, quiet, and communally identified. They all shared a common zeal for better understanding and acting in the social community. A number shared a similar vocational shift in later years, along with so many others then who left the church-based ministry for a secular one.

Shaping the Parish Pastor

On the faculty steering committee for the program was John Fletcher, a moral theologian on the faculty of the Virginia Theological Seminary. John was a still-young, visionary, caustic yet very pastoral person who was moved to take a courageous step. I can remember vividly the moment that decision was made. The Urban Training Program had received a small grant to evaluate its usefulness for seminarians. One clear discovery was that they were constantly tempted to give it low priority because the seminaries did not reward the students' program involvement in the way they rewarded and demanded normal academic course work. When we hypothesized at that meeting a primary reason for this—namely, that it was inevitable as long as the educational goals and process were controlled almost exclusively by scholars rather than pastors and laity—we decided that it would be worth testing out a new model for seminary education. At that moment John looked at me across the table with a sense of the portentousness for him to move in such a direction. For if it was to happen, he would have to quit his job and head up the effort.

After passing tests with various layers of church officialdom, including a number of seminary personnel, the decision was "go." Thus was born Interfaith Metropolitan Theological Education, one of the most bold and tumultuous theological education experiments in a long time. It eventually included students from fifteen Christian, Jewish, and Unitarian faith traditions who were preparing to lead religious congregations. Intermet tried to foster a strong sense of the integrity and mutual enrichment available from these differences. This sense was stretched to racial and sexual differences as well, which had to be explicitly confronted by students.

Much time was spent by students as apprentices with lay and pastor mentors in congregations. Scholars were contracted for specific academic learning needs, on terms felt relevant to the school's core "educational process" faculty and to students alike. Power was balanced along all of the above lines: pastors, laity, scholars, core staff, and students.

After seven valiant years, Intermet died in 1977 largely for financial reasons.[2] It was born at a time of great dissatisfaction with institutional forms throughout the country. It represented one more "larger possibility" of those heady years in the late sixties and early seventies. It died at a time when the cultural climate had become clearly more conservative, and not just economically. A new time of conservation and restoration of divisions between races, faith traditions, nations, and most everything else was rising. Nonetheless, Intermet helped

[2]Its fully evaluated story is available from the Alban Institute, Mount St. Alban, Washington, D.C. 20016 in *Intermet: Bold Experiment in Theological Education* ($7.50).

inspire a reconsideration of pastoral preparation that has had an impact in many other schools, so I know its brief flame did not burn completely in vain. John Fletcher to this day remains a consultant and researcher in theological education (along with his work as social ethicist at the National Institutes of Health); he also remains as a caring godfather for my son Jeremy—an enduring friendship that rose out of those years.

A New Arena for Social Ministry

I remained on the fringe of Intermet's life as a preceptor and supporter. My main arena of activity lay elsewhere. In 1967 representatives of a dozen Washington area faith traditions, Roman Catholic, Protestant, and Jewish, banded together to form the Metropolitan Ecumenical Training Center and asked me to be director.

I sensed that it was time for me to leave St. Stephen's and let my experience there be a basis for helping clergy and laity better understand the evolving social scene and to learn how to more effectively participate in it. I had very little background in training design, though, and very little precedent for what I was asked to do. The board of directors had raised a little start-up money from denominations, enough to last about six months. I had no guidelines for what I was to do or how to go about doing it. This was new for everybody. They just trusted me to do something.

Those are periods that sorely test one's trust in the sustaining flow of grace! I felt very much on my own, needing to make something happen, and fast—or the whole effort would quickly lose its support. I came aboard in the late spring, and with the help of a

curriculum committee of experienced friends that I
desperately and rapidly brought together, a two-
pronged summer program was launched.

The first prong was put to rest forever at the end of the
summer. It was a weekly summer forum; each was
headed up by well-known local religious and political
leaders and focused on various social issues. The poor
turnout taught me that there isn't enough motivation for
most religious people to come out to hear speakers unless
they are very special indeed. Such panels and addresses
can be heard through countless media and in places
throughout Washington, including the neighborhood
bar. Besides, how many people really can identify
significantly with complex metropolitan-wide issues that
cross two states, the District of Columbia, and countless
local jurisdictions? It was just too much to ask.

The other prong was a weekly seminar for clergy
concerned with social issues in their work. The fine mix
of clergy who attended that program laid seeds in my
mind that continued to bear fruit during my succeeding
ten years with METC. It was a group willing to be very
intimate about what was really going on in their
committees, churches, and hearts. No one wasted time
posturing, defending, or hiding. It was a humblingly
gifted time together.

What I began to learn there has become ever more
clear to me over the years; it is out of that later clarity that
I will speak. I became aware of how intricately
interrelated are culture, church, community, and pastor.
Anything inspired or destructive at any level one way or
another will affect the other. You can't simply do
something at one isolated point without it being affected
by whom and how it is done and affecting more than
what you had intended.

This systemic awareness can paralyze action. I

remember reading a marvelously sophisticated report to the Joint Economic Committee of Congress by an anthropologist concerning the intricately complex web of actions that should be taken politically, socially, economically, and attitudinally if significant, durable, needed social changes were to take place in any given urban area. At the end of the report, instinctively sensing the paralyzing result of his analysis, he said something to the effect that, well, just maybe, if neighborhood groups got together and swept their back alleys and a number of other such isolated actions took place, the needed changes would coalesce and happen anyway.

We can't let ourselves be frozen into helplessness by the complexity of it all. But we can't ignore the reality of systemic connections, either. What I learned in terms of the church was the importance of taking seriously its basic unit of the congregation. This is not an isolated unit. But it is an identifiable and approachable one. If the international church is accountable anywhere in particular, it is in the way that basic unit affects the world.

7

The Ministry of the Local Church

If a congregation's internal way of dealing with one another does not embody some modicum of justice, it is likely that its social actions on behalf of the larger community will be distorted accordingly. Maybe the distortion is seen in a paternalism that ignores community empowerment and encourages dependency. Maybe it is seen in the way certain basic issues are ignored and feared in favor of more symptomatic ones. Maybe it is in the way people are subtly exploited. If these are realities within the congregation, how can we expect them to be magically forgotten as members look at their social ministry?

What is said here about the congregation is specifically true for its clergy. If they reflect in their own attitudes and values that which is unjust, divisive, overly controlling, violently fearful of the truth, defensive, and confused, these are bound to affect how they view their own role and the congregation's in the community.

Now all congregations and all clergy are part of a broken world of sin and ignorance. Only in God's good time will it be otherwise. But that "good time" is partly upon us already in Christ, and it is always beckoning us nearer. We are capable of desiring and learning how to listen more closely to the way the Spirit of the Lord is moving among and within us. Then perhaps we will not give the last word to the off-target movements of our own egos when isolated from the true Spirit of God. Brother Lawrence lamented his lost times with the complaint to God, "See what happens when you leave me, Lord?" Of course the Lord never really leaves. We wander away. Then indeed life goes deeply awry. We can learn to pay attention.

Much of my work over the next decade focused on helping clergy, lay leaders, and congregations pay attention in ways that could cultivate a clearer, more open ministry both within the congregation and for the community. The work took a number of forms.

One form was attention to parish clergy. Many of them were bewildered by what was going on in the social scene, or else they were clear advocates of social stances that had led to great conflict with members of their congregations. All were caught up in a historical moment where they were receiving pressures from different sides: on the one side to demonstrate concern for social justice and poverty; on the other to ignore these areas, and instead bring in new members and money (which often was in direct proportion, in white churches, to how socially uncontroversial you could be). Such pressures left the clergy with the tension of discerning priorities among their many roles, ranging from prophetic to private chaplain to the members.

I worked with these clergy personally, in denominational groups, with their lay leadership in congregational evaluation retreats, in the many community group ministries that sprang up in the Washington area and elsewhere at that time, and in an annual METC program that ran over a number of months, a program that eventually focused on clergy new to the Washington area.

That program brought together each year everything that I kept cumulatively learning about what clergy need to pay attention to in the social scene. This included an introduction (through personal visits as well as class descriptions) to the social systems of the area: economic, legal, governmental, media, and the voluntary sector. It also involved some historical sense of how social forces had changed over the years; theological reflection; analysis of the participants' congregations and communities with a view toward planning effective social involvements, as well as planning approaches focused on how the congregation itself might better incarnate a just, reconciled community.

Over the years we also gave more time for the clergy to attend to their own styles of leadership, conflict management, and personal values and dilemmas. I became aware of how rarely clergy had opportunity to speak with others about their own roles and values, in a supportive, open, and challenging context—and how much they needed this opportunity for their own and for their congregations' sakes.

My own focus in those years emphasized political, social, and human relations, inspired by the social prophets and behavioral scientists of the time. That last group was particularly important to me as I sought to develop more competence in understanding the social realities of communities, congregations, groups, and church leadership. I spent many staggered weeks in training conferences with the National Training Laboratories and the Mid-Atlantic Training Committee in those early years at METC, trying to decipher what social analysis can tell us about people, organizations, and communities.

I became particularly enamored with organizational development, a rapidly emerging field focused on the systemic connections of structures, roles, and values in any organization's life and ways of assisting these to move toward more humanly open and managerially effective systems. These learnings have had enormous impact in the operation of business and government organizations and an increasing impact in many churches and other voluntary organizations.

Application of these learnings for understanding and fostering needed social change was suspect in those days by many social activists. In their eyes anything that had emerged out of close work with established structures was tainted with the values of those structures. That indeed was a half-truth. Many basic assumptions of the American economy and social structure, such as the value of certain products, the overarching goals of financial profit, the huge discrepancy in salaries at different levels of organizations, and the social and ecological effects of organizations on the national and international level, were not normally questioned by most of the experts in the field.

However, much attention was paid to certain dimensions that seem essential for a just, human organization: sharing power and influence, treating people in their jobs as whole human beings, not just workers, matching worker skill and motivation with jobs and training—in general, moving toward more effectively democratic and caring places, based on hard data of people's lives and organizational structures.

I was always aware of the inadequacy of this field to the extent that social prophecy was tacitly excluded from such an in-house rational system. On the other hand, I think in many cases more social benefit has come from such a system for more people and has endured than through much of the activity of some fringe social prophets at that time.

Being up-front in an advocate role easily tempts one to mistake hard rhetoric about just social change for the effective system needed to bring change about and sustain it. The organizational leadership of such activists deepened the problem when it was more dictatorial and inattentive to the hard work of careful organizational development than the structures against which they railed. The gift of persons drawn to prophecy, like pioneers in other areas, often seems to be that of shocking people into attention to what belongs to the good of the community which they have ignored or evaded. A second generation of people then is called for who are gifted and willing to attend to the nitty-gritty of institutionalizing the needed changes others have inspired.

In fact, this is just what happened in many cases. Later in the civil rights and anti-poverty movements, much more attention was given to this kind of long haul, less dramatic work. Where this did not happen, initial promise often faded into a morass of incompetent bungling that no amount of rhetoric could rescue. I hope these lessons have been learned well, for the sake of the ongoing really needed actions at every level of social life. Prophecy without this backup becomes maddeningly empty or stillborn rhetoric.

It has always amazed me how organizational leaders can be chosen without reference to their managerial competence, experience, or training, as though it was just something everyone is born with! I am sure we have all suffered under managerial incompetence and power-love enough to know this, yet organizations still often seem to ignore such hard existential knowledge. I have been glad that clergy increasingly are helped to be attentive to this dimension of their work. In the local congregation the pastor's managerial sense is crucial. He/she is pastoral head of what in fact is a very complex and unique voluntary social system.

During those years and since I have been greatly helped by James Anderson, a long-time friend and one of the sharpest people around in terms of local church management, in understanding what a congregation and its leadership are about organizationally. In one of his books, *The Management of Ministry*, co-authored with Ezra Earl Jones (Harper & Row, 1978), he exposes the enormous amount of time that most local church leadership must put into organizational management and what he calls "associational leadership," i.e., helping people relate and move together as a community. Very little energy and time normally are left for more specific spiritual formation: teaching, preparation for sermons, counsel, prayer and other spiritual disciplines, and prophecy.

In the ongoing fragmentation of inherited forms of community—family, stable neighborhoods, community organizations, and so forth—an enormous weight is put on most congregations to be a center of belonging for people. This can far outweigh any more specific spiritual dimensions, especially in liberal churches. I sense at times that the church's specific mission as an expression of the Body of Christ in the world tacitly becomes secondary for a great many people, for whom the church is an expedient basis of belonging and stability. This basis might just as well be some other social organization, if it could provide the same community service.

This reality makes community ministry by the church more difficult. People are often coming to church hungry, tired, wanting love. Given the limited amount of time the church has with people, their motivations become crucial in determining what gets attended.

I have been enormously helped in understanding what the church *uniquely* has to contribute to people on a psychosocial level by the Grubb Institute in Britain, a group of behavioral scientists and lay Christians who have researched the local church for twenty years. I have written about them elsewhere, cf. my *Spiritual Friend* (Paulist Press, 1980) chapter 3. In a nutshell, they see that the local church's primary task, i.e., what in fact it does for people at its unique best, is to provide an arena for right cultivation of their receptive presence to God.

"Right" cultivation means providing ways for people collectively and individually to refresh their souls in such a way that they are fed back into society more energized and free to cope with their own and the society's needs. Behind this view is the theory that all human beings oscillate between a receptive, cleansing, other-dependent, opening quality of consciousness, and an active, managing, intra-dependent quality. The church (or other religious group) in their view is the only social institution accountable for helping people move through the receptive mode in such a way that it is not an escape that ultimately detracts from their capacity to care cohesively with others for the world. With the gospel as its foundation, the church can let people "rest in the Lord" in a way that leads them back into the suffering of the world with the energy and perspective they need.

But this is not the same as spending time in church organizing the action in the world. That action is to be done in unity with others who care, both in and out of the church. The church is responsible for theologizing about all of life, including its social dimensions. But it is not responsible as an institution for the action itself; rather it is uniquely responsible for the management of that side of the oscillation that constantly renews people's *capacity* for coping, seeking justice, building culture, transforming, reconciling action.

The steps of Eucharist are a classic summary of the church's unique way of helping: a relaxed, inviting environment (sanctuary), confession, absolution, the Word, reconciliation in the peace, openness to receiving the enlightening Life of God into us in communion, a corporate environment and widely ranging prayer that keeps our identity "big" (rather than narrowed into a private sense of self), and finally words that move us back toward the world in the dismissal.

There is no magic in this. Much can be warped both in people and in the church's way that blocks a full, open rhythm of receptivity and action. But the point is that attention to this rhythm is essential in human life, and the church is accountable for preaching and teaching its fullness and for helping people rightly pass through its receptive side.

The church cannot do everything. To attempt this is to give in to the temptation of institutional imperialism. The church simply does not have the resources to do it all. Yet because the gospel deals with all of life, it is easy to slip into a confusion between Christian responsibility and the primary *institutional* responsibility of churches. If the church as institution tries to do *everything*, it will likely do nothing very well. If it does not attend to what it *alone* is accountable for in the institutional arrangements of society, then the whole society will suffer. The health, solidarity, and justice of the community is dependent on the church assisting people's receptive mode of consciousness well.[3]

So much more could be said about this challenging and, in my experience, on-target understanding of the local church, but I will leave that to the readings I have referred to and to another book I am finishing devoted entirely to it, from the vantage point of the Christian Sabbath.

Much more could be said also about the endlessly marvelous and yet endlessly frustrating institution of the local church, but I will leave that to those who have made it more of a specialty. I do think it is important to recognize honestly that, for all its functions and possibilities, it is not the *only* institution of the church universal, just as it isn't the only institution of society for attending human need. Not only does the local church need to be free to restrict itself to do what it can most uniquely do well for the *society*, but also it needs to be free to do only *some* of the religious tasks. It can be excellent and unique at assisting people through those rites of passage and crises that face human life: birth, coming of age, marriage, separation, sickness, death. It also is capable, along with the family, of providing a basic spiritual and communal formation. Perhaps the local church's most subtle, and yet very simple special value, is that it is steadily there, visible, available across the land, open, communal, providing a kind of reassurance for human hope in its enduring presence, warts and all.

It should come more as a relief rather than a threat to local churches, though, to remember that the church does have other centers. The family, the "domestic church" (to borrow a Vatican II description), is one. The local church can assist but cannot substitute for this

---

[3]This has been a very broad paraphrase and simplification of a very involved theory. Cf. Bruce Reed, *The Dynamics of Religion* (London: Darton, Longman, and Todd, 1978).

institutional base. It is in the family that so much of the real day-to-day formation (and mal-formation) of Christian life happens.

In Latin America and increasingly in other parts of the world the non-blood "extended families" now frequently called "base communities" have burgeoned. These exist for informal support rooted in scripture, prayer, and reflection about personal and societal life and action in light of the gospel. These are the "ecclesiolae in ecclesia," the little churches in the larger one, that Christian history finds cropping up again and again as places of renewal.

Other groupings provide other bases for the church's life. Associations flourish for special kinds of fellowship, service, prayer, education, retreats, evangelism, liturgy, and the arts. Such groups are often related to the local church, and can be the places, formally or informally, of greatest vitality and real lay leadership within them. Completely separate from the local church are the many celibate and noncelibate covenanted Christian residential communities that often function both symbolically and practically as centers of renewal and radical commitment, with extensive networks of associated people.

The vitality, competence, and versatility of the church depend on the flourishing of these multiple centers of its life, including the local church. It would be dangerous and stultifying to attempt the centralization and control of all church activity in the local congregation, even if it were possible. The Spirit moves when and how it wills. We can discern the authenticity and assist the order of those movements through particular formal representative structures, for the sake of coherence and unity with tradition, but we cannot "blueprint" them into static, preordained centers.

8

The Last Openings:
Justice Pushed a Little Further

Color Justice Inside Organizations

My awareness of the importance of organizational life
as an arena for careful attention led me to spend more
time on race relations *within* organizations rather than
between them in the community. It is within organizations that most people spend most of the waking time:
especially places of work and study. Here people *have* to
live together with people of many kinds, if not all kinds.
It is the basic ongoing testing ground of heterogeneous
human relations. Not only that, the work/study centers
affect the whole society by what they produce or don't
produce in the way of services and goods. We all have a
stake in them.

I "put out a call" in 1968 for people who were
concerned with race relations and who had some
relevant experience with social psychology or organizational development. A large turnout for the meeting at
Howard University revealed how much "race" was on the
mind of the behavioral science community at that time. It
included an amazing cross section of people, some of

whom had a lot more concern than experience. Out of that meeting grew a training program and a network of fifty people, organized into the METC Race Institute.

Over the next eight years these people worked in teams with many schools, businesses, churches, government agencies, and voluntary organizations. Two lessons stand out above all the many others from that rich time. First, it is far more productive to focus on structural inequities and what can be done about them, than it is to focus on attitudes—in other words, to focus on institutional rather than personal racism. Whenever I worked with a group, I almost always spent some time dealing with attitudes. But it became more and more a minority emphasis of the time. Beneath racial attitudes lay a mass of conscious and unconscious experience, fear, guilt, anger, and a host of other confused emotions, usually connected with other things in one's life besides race. In a short time, these deep-seated orientations aren't going to collapse, unless it's a very ripe time, indeed.

On the other hand, as long as you have a modicum of goodwill (along with helpful legal mandates!), you *can* get somewhere together in recognizing built-in forms of discrimination in the overt and subtle ways that an organization is put together. Action plans can be undertaken. Attitudes may be affected positively in time. But whether or not these change, structures that assure more justice can be fostered.

The other major learning from the Institute for me was how beautiful it could be for a cross section of blacks and whites, Jews and Christians to collaborate together both on a human level and a skill level for a purpose that transcended strictly personal gain. Those were the last years of a particularly open phase of American experiment in racial relations. We were part of that time, telling one another intimate secrets and jokes across racial lines that would not likely be revealed today, and sometimes sacrificially caring for one another and for the hope of racial reconciliation. It was a graced time simply "given" us to embrace. We never could have "constructed" those relationships and those opportunities alone. We are so dependent on God's timing and merciful eye, no matter what our understanding and sophistication.

Jews and Christians

The last great opening of those special years for me was between Jews and Christians. By that time most recent seminary graduates had been educated almost universally with a fresh respect for Hebrew scripture—the Old Testament—and were primed for a positive relation to Jewish tradition. On their part, for all their historically well-grounded suspicions, Jewish rabbis and other leaders participated in the general experimental opening of the time and edged toward more collaboration with Christians.

I can remember a young rabbi who participated in our annual program for clergy new to the area. It was a great sign of opening in itself for a rabbi to participate in an intimate continuing education program with Christian clergy. Part of the program included small groups focusing on personal feelings. At one point the rabbi burst into a torrent of anger, aimed at a particular pastor in the group. It was long, long pent-up anger at discrimination by Christians that he had never expressed before to a Christian. As it turned out, there was great healing in that time. The two became close and lasting friends.

Annually we held special Jewish-Christian dialogues focused on various mutual issues. The first was on different views of Israel, with Christians stretching to understand as Jews tried to convey and interpret their strong feelings. These times of special openness were climaxed by a shared METC pilgrimage to the Holy Land together: Jews and Christians, black and white, male and female, clergy and laity.

Most of the Jews on that venture were much more familiar and learned about Israel and the Holy Land than the rest of us—even about Christian sites! It was a jaw-dropping experience to be given a very intimate tour of the Church of the Holy Sepulchre by a rabbi. Seeing the Holy Land through Jewish eyes is to see it through eyes that feel at home. They knew every hill and site we passed that had biblical or other historical reference and pointed them out as though they were showing us their childhood neighborhood, which in a historical sense they were.

It is hard to convey the depth of belonging they expressed. Indeed, such a people who had prayed daily for nearly two thousand years for a return to Jerusalem, who have had perhaps the strongest historical sense of identity of any people, and who have had far more than their share of historical suffering, are bound to revel in the independence of Israel. It is the first nation in which they have ever been a majority since their ancient exile; the first place they could really politically and socially control and secure, after centuries of being in the hostile or barely tolerant hands of others.

That awareness was more penetrating to me than any of the special Christian sites, which I found, for the most part, to be sadly commercialized or scandalously divided between mutually hostile and jealous Christian groups. The one exception was the likely "wilderness" of Jesus' forty-day retreat: the barren hills east of Jerusalem. I was dumbstruck by the utter silence, sharp, clear sky, dry sun, and desertion of all but the most sturdy life forms. There, if I could, I would have stayed and hoped to taste a little of the temptation and strengthening of Jesus and of those

numberless desert fathers and mothers who centuries
afterward lived in Palestine and Egypt, as well as some
who live there today.

The pilgrimage ended together in a new national
forest. There we each planted a young pine tree and
formally dedicated that section of the forest to Martin
Luther King. Standing in a circle, holding hands, we sang
together, "We Shall Overcome."

The graced moment of opening in those years was
beginning to weaken by the mid-seventies. The breach in
the walls of partition were beginning to fill in. One
barrier that rose in the breach was symbolized by a special
day we arranged to explore black and Jewish relations. A
great deal of unexpected mutual misunderstanding and
stereotyping shocked everyone present. People who
thought blacks and Jews were beyond such things were
jolted into the reality of how deep the cleavage was, or
was becoming again, between such strong allies in the
civil rights movement.

Another growing barrier was the issue of the
Palestinians. The hard-line Begin regime in Israel,
together with a growing awareness and sympathy with
the exiled Palestinians on the part of both liberal Gentile
whites and blacks, has left mutual suspicion and distance
between many Jews and Gentiles that is not easily
breached. One small note of hope was the eventual
inclusion of Muslims in our interfaith dialogue and,
eventually, integrally in the organization. But Muslims
did not include Palestinians.

Finally, distance has been created by fewer people
standing together in the breach. A great many Jews and
Christians along with many ethnic groups had begun
stepping back to reformulate their own confused
identities, personalities, organizations, and resources. I
was no exception.

9

Family, Neighbors, and Sexuality

As the seventies wore on I found myself and others exploring and emphasizing the "integrity" of our culture, race, personal identity, sex, and faith traditions. A group of us formed an informal "post-liberal" caucus that met regularly for a year to find our bearings. After the years of expansive social openings in which we had lived and worked, the adjustment to more particular horizons was not easy. But we felt these growing in our bones. We could not continue as we were. Changes were happening in us, as well, and they needed attention.

Family

For me the changes welled up in three major arenas: family, man and womanhood, and faith. My children, Jeremy and Jenny, were growing. What did they need from me? I became convinced that they needed not only my caring attention, but also my convictions about life's purpose and way. I began spending more time with them in family liturgies, scriptural understanding and guidance for their daily life.

My wife Ann needed more. Besides our shared care for our children, she needed me to understand, struggle, and change with her as we both faced the confusion and changes in what it meant to be a man and a woman as the woman's (and man's) liberation movement rose to a crescendo. My continuing way through that liberation is not particularly unique and not worth special attention here. What is worth attention, perhaps, is a vignette from my experience with this movement as it led to the ordination of women in the Episcopal Church.

Women and Men in God

Ann and I shared a highlight of that movement one Sunday at St. Stephen's. The church was packed. Culminating a year of agonizing struggles around the issue of ordination of women was Allison Cheek standing behind the altar in priestly vestments. She was the first woman ever to celebrate Eucharist in an Episcopal church in Washington. As she lifted the bread and wine in consecration, her sonorous, strong voice proclaiming the words of institution, a wave of fresh appreciation washed through me. My convictions about women's ordination before that moment had been primarily intellectual. Now they became fully embodied. I deeply felt the rightness of a woman's complementing the overwhelmingly masculine imagery of God at that time. For that moment it even seemed more natural that a woman was representing the church to God than a man. I am aware that as the imagery of God includes more conscious feminine qualities, the reverse could be said. But then the celebrant represents not just the church to God, but God to the church. Given both of these operational realities, the value of both men and women as ordained leaders can be seen.

The arguments for and against the priestly ordination of women of course are much more involved than this. But these particular dimensions now struck me with particular force. This was true for Ann as well. I think we went home that day with fresh respect for the full place of women in the spiritual leadership of the family of God.

I remember being introduced as a speaker to a large group of Roman Catholic religious educators the week after that well-publicized celebration by Allison Cheek. When the introducer mentioned my connection with St. Stephen's there was a spontaneous cheer. They obviously had been following the Episcopal struggle closely, and seemed as solidly behind the ordination of women as any equivalent meeting of Episcopal educators would have shown itself to be at the time! That incident (and others) put me in touch with how important and encouraging the ordination of women in the Episcopal Church was to many Roman Catholics. Rather than dividing us further from Rome, as many feared, the ordinations I think in fact brought Episcopalians much closer to many Roman Catholics, albeit not the Vatican, and I hope over the long term that will give more support and confidence to them.

The strongest felt argument for ordaining women to me over the years has actually been on other grounds than the imaged symbolic level. Namely, if a woman is graced by God with a deep embodiment of the gospel and a capacity to share this intuitive realization appropriately with others, then she has the right to the legitimation of her leadership in whatever form will assist the use of such gifts. This may not require ordination. Spiritual gifts can be shared through many forms other than ordination by men and women. But it might well include a call to ordination.

Such a deep embodiment of the gospel has not been

the operational standard for ordination with either men or women in our highly rationalized and institutionalized approaches to ordination. But to me it is such embodiment that most counts, and where that is present, I could care less whether it is in a man or a woman's body. Looked at from another angle, the way God has broadly distributed spiritual gifts sexually through history points to how much She/He does care that *both* sexes are called to the full range of possible ministries.

Another dimension of maleness and femaleness before God that has gradually become important to me has to do with the different experience that men and women bring to God: biologically and culturally. This has been a very inadequately explored dimension insofar as it affects prayer life, spiritual disciplines, and spiritual guidance. Perhaps in advanced stages of spiritual maturity such differences fall away in importance. But at least in earlier stages, I think there may be important differences. As more women come to the fore now in spiritual leadership and research, and in honest dialogue with men, the more I hope we will learn about these differences. Understanding them is important for the spiritual ministry of the church.

Through all these new kinds of attention to the meaning of maleness and femaleness in these recent years I, along with many other men, have come to appreciate and affirm my own more receptive, intuitive, and nurturing sides. I sense though that many such men now are in need of help in affirming a constructive place for their *other* sides, which have been so downplayed in liberal religious circles as the stereotypical "feminine" has been more affirmed. I'm thinking here of such stereotypically masculine traits as competition, physical strength, valor, control, provider for others, and rational analysis. Women have been given increasing sanction to reflect these qualities, but I think many men who have been deeply affected by the women's liberation movement have become guilty and uncertain about them for themselves. To the degree such ambiguity reduces the pressure on men to be "macho," these feelings are worthwhile. But they also can cloud the potentially dignified and valuable sides of these traits in the right circumstances for men. The goal, I think, is to allow the full range of traits to be available for either sex, as and when they are really called-forth ways of serving God's glory and authentic community.

Neighborhood

Throughout such changes of the past decade—and changes concerning faith that I will relate in the next chapter—I again found myself grateful for our amazing neighborhood. We have lived in the same house for thirteen years now. We bought it right after the Washington riots following Martin Luther King's assassination. After the riots, many people who could do so sold their houses and moved out of the city. We happened to be ready and able to buy our first house, always a momentous decision for a family (one increasingly fewer families have the privilege of making today). In what kind of neighborhood did we want our children and ourselves to grow up? How do you balance safety, convenience, mix of people, price, and personal values? With just a hint of Jeremiah's purchase of a plot of land in a wobbly Judah as a sign of trust, and the larger motive of really liking that neighborhood and house, we bought into the Adams-Morgan section of the city.

That has remained one of the most volatile, incredibly mixed (racially, ethnically, vocationally, economically, and politically) neighborhoods in the city. Through all of our recent years of narrower focus on family and faith formation, the neighborhood has kept us open and corrected by its full range of human variety. In all the "closures" of the past decade, the neighborhood has remained a sign of hope for us, as well as a realistic sign of frustration, about the human panorama's capacity to make it together under one community roof.

10

The Space Between the Lines: Faith and Contemplative Awareness

My own faith needed attention in the early seventies—for my sake, for my family's, and for my priestly vocation. Indeed that vocation had not meant much for some time. Much of what I did during those action training years could have been done by a nonreligious person. I had reverted back to my pre-seminary days in a way: trusting in the behavioral sciences to teach me what I needed to know: about myself, about churches, about life. A little theological and liturgical overlay gave it all more meaning, but not much heart.

Now, though, this was no longer sufficient. Something was missing. It wasn't the "lines"; the theological words about life were there and seemed adequate. In hindsight, I know it was the spaces *between* the lines: the subtle, unifying, intimate presence that I had not sensed very often, but that now seemed to beckon me.

It had been a long time since I had sensed or even reflected much about that presence in other than its normal human relations form. God was real in words, but distant in intimate awareness. In the dim past there were those moments of vague intimate awareness in Mass

93

as a child, sharpened later in Episcopal liturgies and monasteries. Then there was that strange year of deepening conversion before seminary, and the crowded, testing quality of presence at St. Stephen's. But little else.

Apart from a trusted confessor for several years in Cambridge I had never had a serious spiritual director. I had a daily prayer discipline for many years, but without the help of a director and more personal attentiveness, God and I seemed to keep a kind of static relationship, a negotiated distance. It was steady, but primitive. It was often hard to name God, except in liturgical forms. I abhorred anything smacking of fundamentalism or sentimentality. I knew I would rather be spiritually sterile than false.

I kept a subtle sense of superiority about this. I had balanced theological phrases, and a sound liturgy. That was enough—or at least all I seemed able to bear in those years. God had a way of respecting my freedom, and I trust a way of preparing me for deeper awareness, through those years. I can't help feeling, though, that this deepening was delayed by my own basically fearful inattentiveness.

In any case, some force was pressing up in me now in a way I had not felt since before seminary. And I was not alone. In my work with liberal and moderate congregations I ran into an increasing number of people, clergy and lay, who felt something was missing in their own lives and the congregation's life. They had a very hard time labeling it. Some vaguely felt they needed more scriptural study, or theology, or reflection on their experience, or prayer. Whatever it was, it was not satisfied by their current experience of fellowship, liturgy, preaching, study, prayer, social action, or therapy. All of these were "lines." How do you label the awesome/intimate space between them? And even if you have a glimpse of that space, how do you attend to it without falling into the lines again?

My first glimpse of a way through this came unexpectedly at a national conference of the Association for Religion and the Applied Behavioral Sciences (since changed to the Association for Creative Change) in the summer of 1972. The heart of the three days was given over to forms of meditation led by Toby McCarroll, a renegade Roman Catholic who had formed his own little eclectic religious community in California. He guided us in a variety of Christian and Eastern forms of contemplative presence, and for the first time, I faintly glimpsed what it is to be attentively present *between* thoughts, before the hard lines appear. My few past moments of such presence had come and gone with no framework of practice through which I could yield more fully to the Holy One who is so close in that innocent mutual presence, who indeed forms the real "lines," the real "words," that we see as authentic life in and around us.

Such analysis pushes ahead of my awareness at that time. But I see now where that experience would lead me. It seems fitting that it came through someone on the suspect fringe of the church, in the midst of church human relations and organizational development trainers and consultants, people like myself who in their own way also were on the groping fringe. From this edge, though, the following years would lead me back to what feels like the very Heart of the church, the Heart for which the institutional church is a flickering, often hazy, yet needed channel. This Heart cannot be contained by any institution, for its beat sustains creation itself.

My way toward that Heart was not to be direct. I was moved to deepen the awareness that had begun that summer, but I had little time to pursue it, and resources were few. I attended a few weekend eclectic meditation groups. I sponsored a retreat that explored in a primitive way some Christian and other forms of meditative discipline. I was open, and yet not fully.

I sensed that I was being led down an obscure path that I could not control. Indeed, its very nature involved ever deeper surrender of control. To go further would be far different from accumulating a few new skills and insights to stick onto my flypaper mind. This direction risked an entire disorientation of my life and required trust that a graced reorientation would come, even though its price might be a loss of "self" as I had known and protected it.

The next summer I took a three-month sabbatical leave to sink into this new direction as best I could. Even though many Christians I knew were close to the same sense of reality in their own lives, they were groping as blindly as I was. Christians on the whole had not cultivated careful proficiency in contemplative presence for a long time. Even the leaders of various Christian contemplative communities intimated this reality to me. There was too much dependence on written books and community life to carry the subtlety of contemplative awareness. There was too little of a careful oral tradition passed from spiritual guide to disciple, though Eastern Orthodox tradition in remote places still tries to give weight to this.

I ended spending most of the time so far from Christian tradition as to come around full circle: I worked ten hours a day on contemplative forms of awareness with a Tibetan lama in Berkeley, California, Tarthang Tulku Rinpoché. Everything that I am was given careful attention: body, mind, feelings, intuitive awareness, will, relation to others. All these dimensions were sensitized, alerted, energized, opened, and pressed toward their integral, intrinsic, subtle relation with one another and with a foundational awareness of our graced nature.

This awareness did involve the loss of a long-conditioned sense of a hard, well-defined self. Replacing this loss was a sense of self much more deeply and obscurely defined by God, and much more intimate with the rest of creation. Through Rinpoché's mastery in this process I was paradoxically awakened to Jesus' uniquely called full mastery, at a far more intimate level than I had ever known. I recommitted myself to God as revealed in Jesus Christ late in the summer, on an Ignatian retreat in Pennsylvania.

The details of that summer are in my first book, *Living Simply Through the Day* (Paulist Press, 1978), and I will not repeat them here. To understand my pilgrimage, though, I needed to say at least as much as I did. The months were a spacious watershed out of whose deep waters I still cleanse my vision. For me the waters flow from the same Source as those living waters that Jesus promised would well up to eternal life in the Samaritan woman (John 4:7-30). They fill the spaces between the visible lines of our lives and give authentic life to the lines themselves. When we lose touch with those living waters our vision is clouded and we flounder with one blind step after another.

The whole history of authentic ascetical practice, of spiritual "exercise," is focused on surrendering this blindness to our true Source of life. The discipline, "discipleship," of the spiritual athlete (the Greek *askein*, *ascesis*), is the discipline of laying open all that we are in body, mind, and spirit to those living waters, that the places in us dammed up by deadening sin and ignorance may be offered up for God's cleansing. That cleansing removes the deadening scales from our eyes, so that we might have sight that can really discern the living way. In this broken world, of course, scales return in many devious and obvious ways. Ascetical vigilance is a permanent task.

The vast spacious waters of God seem to well up in graced times through all that is, washing over any ordering forms our minds and traditions create. Where does this leave the particular "lines" of Christian tradition?

It leaves them real, but transparent. God is uniquely embodied in Jesus Christ for us. That is an astounding mystery and an affirmation of faith. Our jammed-up human lines are entered by God and opened to their Source in Christian experience. We are turned around, converted from hard, closed ego lines to permeable, open lines that we know are made of divine stuff, the image of God, out of which all that is real and worthwhile in ourselves flows. Such conversion turns us toward the world with fresh eyes and compassion. We take with us not only our own experience but also the collective lines of the community of faith: its varied experience, interpretation, and ascetical forms. Together these give particular form to a "way" of life, a way with room for our varied personalities and callings.

This way gives us what human beings need to live: structures for sharing, celebrating, acting, and understanding in the light of faith. But the lines of this way are sacraments, not walls. They are doors that allow the living waters to flow and mingle. Far from cutting us off imperiously from those whose lines are different, they free us to detect the living waters flowing through other lines as well, and also the dammed-up blind spots that may be there. We are called to our "way" in Christ. But Christ does not belong to us. Our way we hope and trust is filled with his presence. We are privileged to live and offer that way. But all creation is united in the infinite

Christ. There are no lines in his fullness, or rather, all true lines come out of his fullness.

That is a mystery that spurs me on to look openly at the many ways Christ may be present in the deep religious traditions of this planet. Christians can offer those traditions our sacramental lines to the Lord of life, trusting that a unique gift for everyone lies in them. But perhaps the fullness of that gift not only allows but frees and *requires* us to attend to the fullness of authentic human-divine experience. Deep calls to deep, wherever it is found on earth.

Such an understanding comes out of the years of struggle and exploration that I have been given since that providential summer with Tarthang Tulku. Through the seemingly devious route of the most remote tradition conceivable, Tibetan Buddhism, I was shown in time some of the depths of Christ that I had never known. Scripture, sacrament, and prayer came freshly alive in me. The great "experiential masters" in Christian tradition came to life as well: from the early desert fathers and mothers through medieval German, English, and Spanish mystics to such great paradigms of contemporary pioneering struggle and gifted vision as Thomas Merton, whose own life ended in intimate dialogue with Buddhist teachers.

There is a great dilemma in approaching other deep traditions, though. That is the matter of time. Unless we are scholars or otherwise have great blocks of protected time, most of us simply do not have the luxury of reading and experiencing deeply other religious traditions. As one minister told me, "It will take me the rest of my life to read even the classics of Christian tradition."

So what can we do? Our answer is going to depend on how we sense the Spirit moving in us at a given time, and the resources that are available. Normally I think it is important to gain a *broader* grounding in Christian tradition, especially with those persons who write out of a great depth of experiential intimacy with God. If we read someone out of another *period* of Christian history, it can be almost like visiting another religion; the cultural context is so different that we are confronted with a fresh way of seeing life in God.

This effect also can come from reading about and, better still, visiting a center of renewed Christians living out of a different tradition than our own. For Protestants this might mean a retreat at a particularly alive Roman Catholic or Anglican monastery or retreat center. If we are Roman Catholic or Anglican, it might mean some time spent in an evangelical Protestant center of renewal, such as The Church of The Saviour or the Sojourners community here in Washington. For everyone, it could mean visiting an international center of ecumenical Christian living, such as the Taizé Community in France (or involvement with their members scattered around the world, including the U.S.), or visiting an Eastern Orthodox center, which can be such a different and enriching experience for Western Christians.

Such Christian exploration can be more than enough. The Spirit is with us where we are. We do not *have* to go anywhere else outside Christian tradition for the truth, or even necessarily to the broader Christian experience I have mentioned. However, we can easily become "stuck" where we are. We hear the same words in the same way and maintain the same habits, and instead of becoming sacraments, they can become dulling or narrowing blocks to our realization of the fullness of God's truth in and around us. At such times the Spirit makes us restless, and we sense the need to move out and explore other ways the living water has been channeled.

Sometimes we are moved no further than broader

lines of Christian tradition (keeping in mind what an eclectic tradition that really is after all these centuries of accumulated experience). But sometimes we sense the need to touch that which seems radically different. We need to go far away and see life through a very different window. As such journeys have shown again and again in history, though, we often find in the end that we see the same reality through that window.

In Wales last summer the priest from Brecon told me that what I sought was where I came from. Yet we return with a difference. We see with fresh depth what before had a very flat surface. We are opened to the great divine space out of which the lines of tradition are made. We are less likely to turn the lines into sectarian barriers. They become sacraments with awesome power instead, sacraments of a guiding, mysterious One moving obscurely through all that is. That, at any rate, was my experience. Christian faith was opened up into the vast yet intimate mystery it is; never again could I domesticate it into a little sectarian system. It became a truly "catholic," a "universal" faith that touched all reality.

Perhaps you too are being led toward a "far place" spiritually, that in time will bring you full circle home again with fresh eyes. If you sense this, I would be careful about who and where you choose. Look for a balanced, compassionate, experienced person or place, one that submits to the ascesis, the discipline, of a particular deep tradition's way of life, yet without mistaking the trappings for the substance. Avoid places and people on subtle power trips. Avoid those failing to connect spiritual life and compassionate action for a suffering world. Avoid those allowing no interior criticism or dialogue.

Finally, avoid places and people who are merely eclectic, those who press the fullness of the kingdom without having the equipment, integrity, or readiness for it.

In God's own time, all the lines that are of God will be joined. But that will be "given." It cannot be authentically constructed, any more than Esperanto, an artificially created ostensibly international language, can be constructed to replace our living, organically unfolding languages. Out of a good, universalist motive attempts to bring religious truths together into one religion easily become the rape of all traditions: willful tearing of this and that out of its context and merging it with other pieces equally torn away, forming a patchwork quilt that simply cannot hold together.

However, all really living traditions, by very definition, are always evolving. If we simply malign other religions in defense of some static sense of the eternal, exclusive truth of our own, then we fall into what Krister Stendahl of the Harvard Divinity School recently called a violation of the ninth commandment: "You shall not bear false witness against your neighbor" (which happens, he said, about 80 pecent of the time Christians speak about other religions!). I am convinced that in the organic unfolding happening now in living authentic religious traditions there is a mutual vulnerability whereby each, within the context of its own integrity, is being deepened and broadened. It is in positive yet discerning confrontation with other traditions that each tradition grows toward the fullness of God's truth.

Many Buddhists today, for example, are taking more seriously the implicit social compassion of Buddhist practice in part through exposure to Christian missionary activity. Many Christians, in turn, are taking seriously the neglected, intuitive, contemplative dimensions of the gospel and of Christian tradition in part as a result of Buddhist and other Eastern missionaries in America. I believe this is the work of the Holy Spirit, calling her broader human family ever closer together for purification and wholeness.

This does not mean that all traditions are ultimately the same, or equally true. It means that what *is* essentially the same and true can find mutual reinforcement and fresh perspective, and what is challenged as untrue or incompletely true will have greater opportunity for correction. "Where two or three are gathered together in my name," Jesus Christ promises to be present. Today, that name must be allowed to be more inclusive than Christians at times have been willing to see. For committed Christians it includes the very particular name of Jesus of Nazareth. But Jesus also revealed to us a far greater name, "Son of man," "He who was before Abraham," "the Word from the beginning," "intimate child of the Father," beyond possession or comprehension of any of our lines. Indeed, it is ultimately to protect and share the fullness of this intimate mystery that those lines validly exist at all.

11

Channels for Awareness: Contemporary Spiritual Discipline

I have been struggling with how to "share and protect" the mystery with special intensity since returning from that summer sabbatical leave. As I worked with congregations and clergy seeking to clarify their ministries, I found myself more frequently pressing them to look at their own relation to God with its fears and graced spots.

Liberal churches have had a way of avoiding the intimacy of this question for a long time. Behind this avoidance I have come to see is often their abhorrence of what passes for "spiritual" in American Christian experience, the distortions of originally authentic Pietism and Evangelicalism, stereotyped as blindly emotional, unself-critical, a-historical, anti-intellectual, and privatistic.

The liberal reaction often takes the form of highly conceptual theological and biblical study and preaching, an objective, structured liturgy, and emphasis on social service. An occasional healing or prayer group may spring up around the fringe, but these are never mainline in such churches, and often are seen as a kind of vaguely tolerated and suspect tip of the hat to personal "religious experience" for those who have to have it. Going beyond these to a charismatic group of some kind is just beyond the pale, usually not to be tolerated without resistance if they try to have an undue influence in the church. This reaction can tempt the charismatics toward sectarian extremes rather than mutually correcting exchange.

Of course it needs to be said here that particularly narrow charismatic and other groups often bring such ostracism on themselves when they reflect an imperial attitude toward their way that leaves no room for real appreciation and dialogue with other spiritual paths and scriptural interpretations. I remember the flustered comment of one liberal minister about this situation: "My liberalism presses me to keep a place for charismatic groups in the church, but their conservatism refuses *my* way a place. It isn't fair!"

In such situations we see the longstanding tragedy of the American church: split between distancing intellect and blind feeling, searching rational pluralism and "I found it" sectarianism. Yet what had begun to emerge in my own experience and reading of the tradition was a dimension of "knowing" that simply is not found at either end of these poles. It is the intuitive, self-critical contemplative tradition. I have written about this neglected and misunderstood tradition extensively in my first two books. Here I will only reiterate my sense that it holds the promise of mediating between intellect and feeling in such a way that both of these are given their due, but are kept relative to the deeper, subtler, open mystery of God.

This living mystery ultimately is known through a trusting awareness that is present when we are free of attachment to any seen or felt images of God or self in our minds. Such awareness is of the vast, boundless space out of whose substance the imaged lines of our lives emerge. This space is simply trusted as mysteriously, personally, intimately opened and guided from a Heart beating for us which we can "know" only in total, graced surrender of all we would cling to, even in the end our very image of and self-conscious trust in God. With no idol or isolated independent strength left between us and God, we are free to be who we are in God, from God. Given our broken human condition, such freedom is at best "in and out" with us day by day, moment by moment.

Though such a description of spiritual awareness is very "orthodox," it is gobbledygook if culture and church in fact cultivate a harder sense of self focused on its independent ego preservation and accumulation of goods (material and immaterial). In such a conditioned context, Thomas Merton's view of a human being as a "graced nothing" is just alien and incomprehensible. Nonetheless, I trust that this in fact is what we are in mature Christian experience. Deepening conversion moves in this direction. It is a description of our real dignity and life in God, rather than the pseudo-dignity and life we would concoct for ourselves outside a realization of our human-divine intimacy.

Can such awareness be cultivated? This brings us to the question of an appropriate ascesis, an authentic spiritual formation practice, for our time. It is an enormous question. The answer involves sensitivity to different personality types, callings, and social situations. It also involves sensitivity to people's scars, illusions, and sins dragged into the present that bring with them a trail of false enthusiasms, fears, confusions, doubts, evasions, and yearnings. These can be seen in the highest leadership positions of the church as well as in the statusless lady in the back pew who shows up once a year.

No one is exempt from obstacles and resistance, just as no one is exempt from the hunger for true self and true community in God, a hunger that never leaves us until satisfied. Indeed, this is our most basic human drive. We may sublimate it in different ways. But it is the deepest hunger for which we were born to find food.

What is clear is that the Christian community on the whole does not provide an adequate, developmental means of feeding this central yearning in us, even though that is what it is essentially for. Those confused, willful barriers in us distort the gospel that is offered. Much too many sweets are given; far too little bread. Francis de Sales once said that we are in danger of wanting the honey without the bread: the good feelings, womby fellowship, tranquilizing strokes.

The bread is authentic spiritual awareness. This always is gifted, but part of the giftedness is built into our very natures. This is why spiritual disciplines are and always have been important. They knead the stiff dough of our lives, make it porous for the Spirit, keep it malleable, and bake it, so that it might become the bread of life for others, as we are called to share our substance. Disciplines provide an environment for the image of God, the "graced nothing" we are in God, to appear, be recognized, and become more powerful and steady in our lives.

What are some of these disciplines that need to live in us and our churches today?

Some of them do live fairly widely in churches, especially corporate worship, Bible study, a mutually caring and celebrative fellowship, and forms of service. Each of these, however, has a way of becoming shallow, artificial, culture-bound, and distorted when not undergirded by more intimate disciplines that attend the unique ways God's grace is streaming through our individual and corporate lives, and the ways we are cooperating with or resisting that stream.

Such "attending" historically is called spiritual discernment: discerning (to use the classical Christian description of it) what is of the Spirit in our lives, what is of confused or sinful ego, and what perhaps is demonic. Some people, according to Paul, have a special gift of discernment. In the early church thousands of people streamed to the deserts of Egypt and the Near East to find a desert father or mother, because many had reputations for this gift.

With these spiritual pioneers, though, it becomes clear that this gift of discernment to some extent belongs to us all. This partially hidden gift inherent in our nature was cultivated in the desert through a radical devotion to a life of spiritual combat with all that is not of God. This life, to the degree that it was authentic and called, unfolded the "clear eye" of discernment in them. Such an eye ultimately is graced, a gift of God. But God cannot give steady sight to an eye full of confused, grasping, crowded images. Ascetical practice, spiritual discipline, prepares the way of the Lord, so that we can truly receive, integrate, and utilize the gifts given, especially the wise "eye of discernment."

The more intimate disciplines that cultivate this openness are manifold. No single set of them can be defined for everyone as part of a modern discipline. What is right at a particular time for us depends on many variables in our lives. Three foundational "intimate" disciplines, though, I have found to be of vital importance for many people at some time in their lives. They need to share a common motivation: the realization of the Severely Loving One in all things.

Ministry and Sabbath

The first discipline involves a disciplined rhythm in our lives, one that oscillates between active doing (ministry) time and receptive being (sabbath) time. As I mentioned earlier, I believe this to be so important for our contemporary situation that I am now writing a separate book on it, related to the historic Judeo-Christian sabbath day, and I have alluded to it in my previous books.

This rhythm is the Christian form of a basic human rhythm that we cannot escape. The question then is not *whether* we move between action and rest, but *how* we do this. Historically, for Christians, this involves a significant block of time where in various ways we attentively rest in the Lord: the classical, often distorted Christian sabbath. That time of sheer appreciation of life in God, of receptivity to the graced quality of all life, overflows into an active, attentive caring for life.

This contrasts with the more normal recent rhythm of life in American and other highly industrialized and urban cultures: one that moves between narrow escape and driven work. That rhythm risks a quality of drunken mind all the time, a mind privatized into isolated ego concern, and fragmented between a rest that escapes our deeper reality in God and work that is unconnected with the unity and hope of life that overflows true sabbath time.

The churches have an enormous, unique opportunity and responsibility to embody and witness to the rhythm that best expresses the reconciled receptive-active modes of presence that are inherent to life in Christ. Such a rhythm has been lost or shrunken by most churches, out of their historical distortions of it and out of the pressures of the culture's alternative rhythm. One of the most important steps needed in the 1980s I believe is exploration of ways to restore this rhythm to individual and corporate life.

I have experimented in my own personal and family life with such an alternative rhythm. It is possible despite our unsupporting environment, and it is an enormous relief from enslavement to the destructive blindness of the culture's frenzied way. It is a rhythm that both teaches and expresses the gospel: the gifted, unitive, intimate, inviting power of God through all dimensions of our lives. Though possible for us, such a rhythm is not easy; it is not likely to be sustained for long without the support of others. It will require an experimentation in form related to our particular circumstances and personalities, and a certain flexibility as our circumstances change.

My family tries to assure a sabbath quality of time that, at its fullest, begins with dinner on Saturday evening and concludes with sundown on Sunday. We have evolved welcoming and closing rituals influenced by the Jewish Sabbath that mark off the time as "different." We try to keep work and worry to a minimum during that time, and appreciation of life as it is in God to a maximum. This is cultivated through especially good meals, candles, play, music, scripture, worship, quiet times, stories of hope, and anything else that seems helpful in setting off the period as especially receptive to life's giftedness.

I am particularly concerned that our children are conditioned to appreciate this different quality of time. Their lives are filled with great pressures to produce, achieve, and conform. At its best, such time points to their calling to ministry and community. But this is only the second half of our calling in God. The first half is a calling to an end-in-itself joy in life, as gifted and

unmerited from the One who created us for the sheer
love of doing so.

True ministry emerges from this awareness properly
grounded, and less prone to the violence and idolatry of
works-righteousness. Energy for truly called work in no
way suffers from this awareness. Indeed, with it we can
discern clearer what is truly called work, and what is
simply our attempt to justify ourselves; what is work out
of our appreciation of God's love for us, and what is work
out of self-contained fear and desire.

Sabbath and ministry flow into each other in countless
ways every day, especially as we become old and less
production conscious. When the reign of God is full, the
poles of the rhythm will become one, as they are always in
God: perfect-rest-in-motion. Until that fullness of time,
though, our condition calls for an intentional rhythm of
sabbath and ministry.

Sabbath time in this rhythm is needed not only on a
special day of the week, but as a "mini-sabbath" for at
least a few minutes each day, and as a "maxi-sabbath" in
multiple-day retreats or other such receptive appreciation times each year.

Personal Prayer

The second foundational discipline involves our
personal prayer. Until eight years ago that meant for me
primarily two things: saying/singing the formal words of
liturgies and a rather mechanical intercessory prayer for
others. I don't think there was much sense of the real
efficaciousness of prayer or of intimacy with God.

It is amazing how well our ways of prayer reveal our
images of God. Despite my mouthing all the right
theological words about God's presence with us, in fact
my relation to God was either intellectual or, in crisis

times, pleading-emotional, yet without deep, steady confidence or trust. As I think is true of many people conditioned in liberal theological traditions (and many in conservative ones, too), a streak of "Pelagianism" ran through my middle: i.e., the heresy that much more of my own and the world's salvation depend on my willed independent action than on God's intimate inspiration.

This classic "works-righteousness" is very powerful in American life. From it stems our tendency toward moralism and our suspicion and frequent ignorance of receptive intimacy with God. Gregory of Nyssa, one of the most influential of the early church fathers, well said that we all have both an "ontological" relation to God, i.e., an end-in-itself son/daughtership, and a "moral" relationship, an active caring in life which overflows from an image of God that our son/daughtership expresses. These are the two dimensions of our calling that I earlier affirmed. One of the great values of sabbath time as I have described it is precisely its focus on our gifted, simply-to-be-appreciated "image of God-ness." In such time we touch directly that bottomline purpose of creation: the sheer joy of it, like the sheer joy of just being a family at its graced best. Out of that intrinsic intimacy flows an awareness of life in God. Our prayer after such awareness is never the same.

For me that awareness came through regular meditation periods, focused primarily on mind and body cleansing/opening exercises that would leave me simply present, appreciative, and with a permeable, light sense of "self." (I describe some of these in *Living Simply Through the Day*.) When that lightness is there, our sense of God shifts. No longer is it a hard, insider-outsider, distant, opaque relationship. It shifts rather to a much more co-inherent, fluid, intimate, yet obscure one.

The depths of prayer shift to silent mutual presence, as

in the depths of any true love relationship. In such moments it is possible to glimpse what I think Merton means by human beings as "graced nothings." This description is not a put-down of human strength and freedom. Rather, it merely describes what is experienced and known about the utter intimacy of our real strength and freedom with God's.

In time old forms of "active" prayer—intercession, petition, confession, thanksgiving, and praise—returned spontaneously to me during meditation. But it was not the same as before. Surrounding and in the middle of such active prayer was an infinitely spacious, intimate, personal Mystery out of which the words came and into which they dissolved. The words were the "lines" that gave particular shape to the vast spaciousness of God. Such pleading, cleansing, grateful words were expressions of our dignity in the image of God. In that image we are called to share freely in reverberating the divine reconciling energies that reveal the kingdom.

Such prayer needs to be a regular practice. We easily cover over who we really are in hustle-bustle days. We need room to settle down regularly to prayer, so that our hustle-bustle has a little more chance of emanating clearly from its intended Source, rather than blindly from the confused desires/fears of surface self.

Separate times for prayer are not meant to be dualistic. They do not contact and define a different reality from that of the rest of the day. On the contrary, they allow us to know the unity of the day, the weaving together of God, self, and others through whatever happens. In such allowance for the way things really are, we also sharpen our eye of discernment, which sees more clearly what has been merely the ego chaff of the day, and what the real kernel.

In time such special prayer periods seep into the day. I

have found myself praying spontaneously for and with people as the day unfolds. And space has appeared in the middle of my active, crowded ego self that lightens my grasping.

Sometimes doubt and frustration come. I feel the helplessness of my prayer along with my striving, fearful heart. I wait out these times on naked hope alone. They are simply givens in a broken world marked by such a loose, easily short-circuited connection with Reality. Then we know best how much we need one another's prayer and fidelity. The Body of Christ is very real. Our own prayer then becomes more skeletal discipline than heart. Yet it is very much needed in such times. It bears our hope.

Sometimes even the hope is buried; there is nothing left in our weakness but the One who secretly carries us. "Where can I escape your Spirit?" We cannot, thank God. Our habitual prayer reminds us of this, even in the seemingly worst of times.

The strength of such a prayer discipline is very relevant to our social ministries. In it is that perspective that saves us from becoming attached to our own schemes for social salvation. At the same time we are saved from despair, lethargy, and narrow vision. Our prayer guides us toward solidarity with God's movements in and around us. At least, that is one fruit of authentic prayer. So many activists of the sixties learned this lesson in the seventies. They are the ones who can be trusted to endure in the eighties.

Spiritual Direction

The third foundational personal discipline I have experienced with special importance for our time is spiritual direction. The practice of spiritual direction involves allowing ourselves to attend the hidden stream of the Spirit in our lives with another person, at regular intervals. It is a time when together we set our interior camera lens on "infinity," seeing our lives not in terms of problems to be solved, but of a nudging Mystery to be appreciated *through* our problems, through all that we are and all that is.

Spiritual direction (or friendship, companionship, mentorship, guidance) assumes our intent to be accountable to God for our attentive responsiveness to the Spirit's movements in and around us, and for discernment of "lesser" spirits that we can confuse with that true movement: lesser powers of ego striving/fearing, or even of demonic influence.

Such accountability involves commitment to a way, a structure of life that includes the rhythms of sabbath, ministry, and prayer I have mentioned, along with some form of those general historic disciplines of the church: corporate worship, scriptural reflection, fellowship, and service. Accountability may involve other disciplines as well, such as fasting, journal-keeping, and forms of meditation.

With a spiritual friend, appropriate disciplines for attentiveness can be decided upon, in the context of our current readiness, needs, and temptations to evasion. Our spiritual friend is present over time with our unique journey in faith, as part of the larger corporate journey of faith that we all share. He or she is not our private therapist, but our public icon: a window through which we see our whole life and its graced calling in a whole creation called to the fullness of God.

I have been in a very steady spiritual direction relationship now for eight years, after a lifetime of at best occasional and mostly casual relationships. These monthly hours have been a great gift. They have felt like a thin, stable human link to my real being and calling in God. Without that relationship I think I would have been seriously out of touch many times with the grace of God happening so near at hand.

I have been graced with a particularly right director for me. It has been an unusual relationship in that I seem to be right for him as well; we are in a *mutual* direction relationship (though each of us is director and directee at clearly different times). We pray for each other daily: that perhaps is more important than our physically present time together.

This ancient Christian discipline is ripe for wide-scale attention today. No longer can the church "carry" serious Christians through a lifetime solely through its general guidance of corporate worship, sacraments, sermon, study, and fellowship. Both church and culture are so full of conflicting values, and so fragmented and emaciated in terms of communal formation, that almost everyone needs someone with whom to sort out their life in the Spirit at least for certain periods of their lives.

Life in the Spirit is a dynamic, subtle, surprising life, moving from Paul's *napioi*, babes who need to be fed with milk, toward *teleoi*, those wise in the Spirit. Personal spiritual guidance over time symbolizes and empowers our attentiveness to this lifetime process. Encouraging its spread encourages an awareness of a lifelong process of sanctification that challenges a static sense of life in the Spirit. Such a static view can be mistakenly derived from the many churches where expectation of members focuses on church attendance and service, and perhaps on a conversion experience, but where there is no real expectation of a lifetime's conversion process, and ways of assisting its nurture.

Even in times when the church and culture seemed more capable of corporate guidance through such avenues as sacraments, study, and the modeling of the fellowship, serious Christians still sought out individual assistance for their paths. The validity and need of spiritual direction thus has always been present. Only today it is more vitally needed than ever.

Much of my time in the past few years has focused upon understanding this ministry. It is one that is always happening informally between people. All of us are called upon at one time or another to provide such a presence for others. Some people are especially gifted in this.

This ministry, though, can easily become confused and dissipated by falling into counseling-oriented ego-coping, problem-solving modes, where attention and surrender to God through all things no longer is central. It also can be more inflexible and more limited in historical and experiential perspective than necessary.

With this in mind a group of us began in 1978 an experimental two-year, part-time program for the support and further education of people called to this ministry. It was based at the Washington Theological Union, with the initial sponsorship of the Association of Theological Schools. My second book describes this program, along with a historical and practical introduction to spiritual direction (*Spiritual Friend*). The demonstrated need for such a program, for both laity and clergy, has led us to continue it now on an indefinite basis.

I also have found myself a go-between for hundreds of people seeking a spiritual guide in the Washington area. A great many people are ready to take the leap into this intimate discipline if given the opportunity to be with someone they can trust. They normally do not need (and are not likely to find) a real spiritual master. Such persons are graced rarities that cannot be "trained." They are given to a society only a very few at a time (probably all

God thinks we can absorb!). But there are many gifted persons who, though not masters, have a depth of faith and attentiveness with us that is enough for what we need.

My own little experience with Buddhist spiritual guides convinces me, as Thomas Merton once said, that Asian guides (at their best) have more carefully attended the subtle development of human spiritual consciousness than we normally have in the West. We have much of potential value to learn from their ways of experientially passing on the "intuitive awareness" of the tradition's truth. We are so analytically or affectively geared in our approach to life and people that we have little experience in how to pass on such awareness.

I remember facing Korean Master Seung Sahn once in the Zen form of personal spiritual guidance: "dokusan." This normally is a brief interview during which time the teacher in effect tests how much you have intuitively realized the truth, or how much you are still "outside" it, in concepts that have not yet been really "embodied." Seung Sahn placed two different objects before me. While holding the perennial "stick" of a Zen Master, he said, "Are these two objects the same or are they different? If you say they are the same, I will hit you thirty times. If you say they are different, I will hit you thirty times. Now what is your answer?" (The threatened blows, by the way, are symbolic not literal with him!)

Such a question is designed to stop your "figuring-out," conceptual mind, and to encourage your intuitive realization. This requires total involvement in the question: your whole body, mind, feelings, intuition—everything must "die" into it. You must *become* the question so thoroughly that there is no "you" left over thinking/feeling about it. Then the "embodied" answer can be manifest.

In this case the answer might involve slapping your hand against the floor. The answer is beyond a subject-object dualism, and it is beyond a "they're both the same" monism. A slap expresses the "unity in diversity" that the objects are to intuitive awareness. But this must be more than a concept. A real Zen Master can tell whether your answer really is more. If it is not, she or he will send you back for more meditation, or some other discipline for attentiveness.

I think that such a process adapted to Christian practice could help us attend a subtle firsthand embodiment of the gospel, rather than attending only to a secondhand conceptual understanding of something "out there," or a seeming firsthand *feeling* that easily confuses ego-desires and fears with the special presence of God. Such spiritual guidance can help mediate what I earlier lamented as the Western polarization between critical intellect and blind feeling.[4]

In doing so, it can bring alive experientially the truth behind much Christian doctrine that seems irrelevant to so many. For example, I think the question asked by Master Seung Sahn in a Christian context tests our "orthodoxy," i.e., our embodiment of true Christian experience. To have responded with the answer, "the objects are different," as a sufficient answer, leaves one asserting an ultimate dualism that does not express the subtlety of "graced unity in diversity" at the heart of Christian experience. The behavioral outcome of such a view is likely to approach a Pelagian heresy, i.e., since things are *ultimately* different from one another; extended to include ultimate distinctions between our-

---

[4]The Japanese Jesuit, J. K. Kadowaki, has written a very provocative comparison of Zen awareness with the awareness and methods of Jesus in his *Zen and the Bible*, (Routledge & Kegan Paul Ltd., 1979).

selves and God, then it is up to us through our works to *will* life into active being. It is not the intimacy of grace happening through us. It is our own ultimately separate action.

On the contrary, if we had answered, "the objects are the same," we would be left asserting an ultimate monism that again does not express the subtlety and fullness of Christian experience. The behavioral outcome of this view is likely to tend toward a Quietist heresy: i.e., since ultimately there is no distinction between things, including between us and God, then all we have to do is sit back and let God happen; there is no real human freedom and cooperation.

Orthodox Christian interpretation does not so reduce and distort the truth into less than it is (one definition of "heresy"). Rather it involves an interwoven divine-human flow that moves between these twin "traps" of over-separation and over-integration. It is a life-path marked by an *attentiveness* that discerns this flow and its lapse into one or other of the traps. It is neither a "doing" (Pelagian) nor a "being" (Quietist) path; it is a co-inherent attentiveness between these. A rhythm of sabbath and ministry time in this context allows an active or receptive attentiveness; it is not meant to infer any ultimate distinctions.

My guess is that in every sixty seconds most of us fall into one or the other of those traps over half the time! A spiritual guide, and the guidance of authentic spiritual disciplines, can aid us in discerning when this is happening and allow our energy and prayer to aim for that sharply aware path down the middle where we are less likely to miss or refuse the grace that appears.

12

A Center for Pilgrimage

As I found myself offering more and more conferences and groups related to spiritual formation, my managerial instinct told me that more organizational coherence was needed. A shotgun of unrelated fragments is fine for an exploratory stage. But there comes a time when you begin noticing emerging patterns that cry out for a framework that gives understanding and direction.

This is always a dangerous moment. It is the time when American entrepreneurship can take off and let organization become an end-in-itself. I am forever thankful to the spirit of iconoclasm in those friends I gathered to consider an organizational form. They resolutely resisted any temptation to form a self-justifying, pretentious movement or other hard sense of shared identity. Indeed, they spent much time humorously pricking any rising bubbles of latent elitism or esoteric knowledge, focusing instead on our own often blind groping and empty-handed prayer.

The upshot was an agreement that we were called to an organized "something" as framework for our collective concerns, but that "something" needed to be light and permeable by the Spirit. Dolores Leckey, a good Roman

Catholic friend, shared with us the nature of a medieval pilgrimage. This pilgrimage was something that people joined when they were ready and left when they were ready, upstaging no established religious structures, but rather providing potentially fresh breezes of life for them, from outside their insular forms. This image struck us as right. We chose a name inspired by Tom Murphy, a fellow METC staff member, that expressed the goal of the pilgrimage: *Shalem*, Hebrew for movement toward wholeness, fullness, completeness in the Lord.

Shalem was dedicated in a chapel of the Washington Cathedral by a motley band of humanity in 1975. Its early years, especially its learnings about ways of working with long-term groups focused on contemplative awareness and vocation, were chronicled in a book written by a close friend and colleague, Gerald May, *Pilgrimage Home* (Paulist Press, 1979).

Behind that book lay two years of reflection by a small research team enabled by a small grant from the Lilly Endowment. The sociologist on the team, Parker Palmer, emboldened us to let a basically intuitive research method guide us.

Several years before I had tried to pursue a little more "objective" approach, focused on data gathered from outside our own experience. With another research team, a number of laypeople were interviewed and asked about their spiritual journeys. The team then tried to reflect on the results in terms of certain criteria for spiritual maturity, and in relation to different denominational and other objective data (the summary is still available from the Alban Institute, Mount St. Alban, Washington, D.C., 20016, under the title: *Spiritual Growth, an Empirical Exploration*).

I learned the limits of approaching spiritual life as an "outsider" from that experience. It was a watershed for me. I became determined more than ever to explore that life as an "insider." I knew that it would be my own developing interior awareness that would be the best teacher. The spiritual life is water that simply cannot be understood without jumping in. From the outside, you can only guess, and paint pictures. These can have value, but they never can substitute for your own plunge.

My fascination with the behavioral sciences cooled once again. They could be important adjuncts, correctives, and aids to direct, personally surrendering faith and discerning experience, but they could never more than weakly surround that to which we are all called: a *firsthand* in-touchness with life's sin, ignorance, ambiguity, gracedness, and callings. Novels, biographies, and the writings of spiritual masters spoke to me more adequately of such firsthand awareness than scientific or speculative theological texts, though I continue to value these.

As part of the "Pilgrimage Home" project I interviewed a number of spiritual leaders in North America and Britain concerning their understanding of spiritual development. One of these exposed clearly a residual streak of "outside researcher" in me. It was with Master Seung Sahn, the Korean Zen Master earlier mentioned. When I asked him, "What is Zen?" he responded with a big smile, "Why do you want to know?" Suddenly it dawned on me that behind my questioning was a lack of confidence in my own firsthand spiritual awareness, and Seung Sahn discerned that. He also knew that he could never give me that awareness. The outside observer cannot borrow it from someone else. Each of us must die our own death to illusion and sin and trustingly await full embodiment of grace.

That experience allowed the necessity of firsthand spiritual awareness to sink in still deeper, along with an awareness of the many ways I try to evade this truth. I still see my evasion at times, not just with others in person, but with others in books. I do not salivate quite the way I used to as I open some old classic or new title, but there still are those unalert moments when I expect that someone else will reveal the truth for me. Each book can become a new subtle hope for this, another grasping outside for what can only be realized through naked presence.

Spiritual reading historically was never meant to take the place of one's own firsthand confrontation with demons and angels. All it can do is surround us with hints, warnings, methods, guidelines, and encouragements. Each of us, as the theologian Martin Thornton once said in relation to Anglican tradition, is an experiment in continuity. Robert Lechner, a Christian philosopher, reminded me recently that it is a very recent broadscale discovery that to be human *is* an experiment. As he says, this is an insight that is "for keeps" now, and it applies as much to religious experience as to any other.

We cannot give up this insight. We cannot borrow someone else's experiment nor successfully recreate a folk culture that closes down experiment. God made each of us as a unique experiment in loving, suffering, delight-filled potential. But in Christian experience we are surrounded by a cloud of witnesses, past and present, in whose communion our unique expression of the one journey is grounded and subtly guided. We are never alone, except in our willful, self-isolating moments.

By 1977 I became clear that Shalem was a full-time calling. I could no longer do justice to that institute and responsibly remain director of METC, with its much broader focus that included clergy and parish development and many concrete social issues. I had hoped that these three often divided areas: social issues, technical clergy/parish development, and spiritual development could remain together symbolically under one umbrella. They in fact are different facets of one reality, and I think they need one another's mutual correction and enrichment. But that was not to be. In January 1979 Shalem became an independent Institute for Spiritual Formation. As it turned out in God's surprising grace, that independence has allowed many good things to evolve.

The transition to that new phase was not easy. When I realized that I would have to leave the larger umbrella organization and develop an independent base, I did not know how or whether I should do that. I spent many agonizing days trying to discern a right direction.

I was sure of only one thing: a call to some kind of full attentiveness to spiritual formation. It was also clear to me that I needed a deeper grounding and confidence in the history and development of Christian ascetical and mystical tradition for such a full-time ministry. So while continuing to listen for specific vocational direction, I enrolled in the Union Graduate School's Ph.D. program (part of the Union of Experimenting Colleges and Universities) while continuing to work part time.

I am proud of that doctoral program, for all my frustrations with its many little weaknesses. That I had to turn to a secular-based program in order to get a degree that would combine experiential and academic development is symptomatic of the Western church's split of these areas. There is simply no educational center in the church to my knowledge that offers a careful integration of intellectual, affective, and intuitive ways of knowing at the highest degree level. The Union Graduate School offered that opportunity, not so much because of a particular commitment to this specific integration (though this is encouraged), but because of its commitment to provide an alternative higher education model for persons with enough experience and maturity to develop a contract that *allowed* such integration. Indeed, the knowledge split just mentioned is even more powerfully apparent in most secular higher education institutions than in the religious schools. It is a common Western disease.

The doctoral program tried to do for mature students one of those things that Intermet Seminary tried to do for seminarians: i.e., to allow more dignity, influence, and initiative for students in the educational process. Each degree contract arranged between student and faculty was mutually negotiated in relation to past experience and exact needs of the student for proficiency in a particular field. The contract also must include a clear indication of social relevancy and some dimension of needed personal growth.

As such it moves toward a holistic degree program. This is pressed further by its required exposure to other student projects in seemingly totally disparate fields, because of the school's assumptions about the integral nature of human knowledge, and the distortions of over-specialization. Such holistic assumptions to me are very conducive and natural to a Christian view of life. Unfortunately, American theological schools have come to so model themselves upon secular professional higher education schools that they frequently lose this holism in both method and content.

I do not fault the schools for this. Rather, I think it is symptomatic of a centuries-in-the-making internal split in the church's consciousness between different ways of knowing God. There also is the simple reality that one person can only learn and be exposed to so much in a given period of time. Categories of learning are built into the human ordering of life. Yet these categories can be much more intentionally cross-fertilized than they have been allowed to be in higher education. If educational centers of the church instead ignore this opportunity and reinforce divisions in our ways of knowing God, they will in effect impede the full embodiment of the gospel.

Before finishing my Ph.D. it had become clear to me that I should stay in Washington and try to launch Shalem as an independent entity. When we received a two-and-a-half-year foundation grant through the Association of Theological Schools in the U.S. and Canada to focus on that "integral" dimension of learning known as spiritual formation, I knew we could get off the ground.

In these past three years of working with theological school faculty, I have become aware of the great ferment, confusion, and hope that exists in a broad cross section of theological schools concerning spiritual formation. My own confidence is that this area holds promise of bridging those polarized ways of knowing God that have so crippled and warped the church's awareness and mission.

Shalem's office sits atop Mount St. Alban in Washington. When I look out my window over this city that summarizes so much of America's deep corruption, massive power, and great promise, I wonder what possible difference Shalem, this small drop-in-the-bucket of an organization, can possibly make.

Alone, of course, it is nothing. My hope and trust, though, is that Shalem is but one manifestation of a widespread yearning for deeper spiritual formation today. Its special little place in that collective yearning and its fruits slowly unfold (though not without our own inevitable brands of blindness and willfulness).

What Shalem and all of us are called to be now involves many assumptions about the nature of our very complex world in the years ahead. I have no crystal ball for envisioning that world. But I have shared a few hunches about some things that are important for us to attend. Let me carry these a little further now.

13

Envisioning the Future

"Just go straight!" That was a favorite phrase of Master Seung Sahn in my time with him. "Straight" meant letting yourself be fully embodied between those traps of dualism on the one side, with its tempted works-righteousness, and monism on the other, with its tempted passivity. Isaiah for me allegorically proclaims this, too, in his great Advent theme: "Make straight in the desert a highway for our God. Every valley shall be lifted up [our passiveness], and every mountain and hill be made low [our works-righteousness]" (Isa. 40:3-4).

John the Baptist picks up this cry and connects it with repentance: a change of heart, a cleansing of the cloudy eye, so that the saving truth can be realized in the face of Christ, that personal face of the Holy One who uniquely affirms and empowers our divine-human history. Jesus tells us the price of this realization: the death of attachment to our illusory willfulness. He takes this death upon himself for us, cutting a straight way between two thieves who have fallen.

Before us in the years ahead are a great bewildering host of possible "ways." Our pluralism has never been greater. These ways only occasionally touch the gifted straight path. That is the nature of a yet-to-be-fulfilled world, where all of us live at best with only a loose electrical connection to our Source. The light goes on and off; we never steadily have that sound eye of the body Jesus spoke of, without which all is darkness and we lose the path.

We have some beacons: scripture, tradition, human experience, our contacting faculties of reason, feeling, intuition, and willing, and the guidance of one another. We also have some sirens that have brought us onto the rocks before: all the deadly sins, illusions, and confusions to which each of us is susceptible. Where we have succumbed to these in the past without repentance or awareness, we drag into the future not only our susceptibility to them, but a hard trajectory, an entrainment of patterns that will pollute what we touch.

Our first priority for attention in the time ahead, as in all times, needs to be our own deepening repentance and awareness. Jesus spoke of first removing the beam from our own eye before worrying about the speck in our neighbor's. If there is anything that the personal receptive mode of attention so prevalent in the past decade has taught, it is how much pollution (along with grace) comes out of us and affects our vision and action. That was a needed corrective to the previous decade's heightened awareness of the pollution that comes into us through misshapen social structures and arrangements.

Our correlative attention is to those social structures and arrangements. That is half of what a freshly cleared vision is for: to attend the justice and care of our neighbor (including nature). The other half of a clear eye is simply to enjoy our neighbor, thereby reflecting the nature of God who multiplies Being for the sheer joy of it.

We bring this two-edged Christian vocation into the years ahead as we bring it into every period of history. Yet each period has its own need of weighting differently the many possible forms of compassion and joy. Each of us will envision the needed weighting in terms of our own limited evolving experience and sight. The remainder of these pages will summarize a few selected concerns that I think are particularly important in the coming years.

There are many concerns that are important and not neglected (at least in print) in the sight of many in the church, including those who have written before me in this "Journey in Faith" series. I will not repeat these, because others have spoken to them with insight and sophistication. I could only give unnecessary variations on their themes. I refer here especially to the various facets of the struggle for justice, social responsibility, and ecological stewardship among races, classes, sexes, economic and political systems, and cultures.

The Body of Christ is fully present only *between* us and our many different weightings. Full humanity is never adequately represented in any of us singly. We need the humility of sitting under one another's experience, along with confident assertion of our own and a common sitting under the Head of the Body in whom alone the fullness of life is known. Without such a view we are in danger of succumbing to single issue and single group myopia.

Unity in Diversty

I have spoken of the first task as removing the beam from our own eye. That beam is enlarged by a culture which asserts in every way possible that basic reality is "me" or "us," isolated individuals or groups with a frequent sense of inner impoverishment that must be fed compulsively on things, achievements, people, education, security.

The hard dualism set up between an individual (or collective) sense of ego reality and the rest of reality colors and shapes our attitudes and actions. The valleys of our isolated inner emptiness often lead us to strive not for a graced straight path, but for a mound of grasping, self-willed achievement. We fall from one trap into the other, from passive depression into mindless activism, missing the subtle way reality in God cuts through these traps with a discerning freedom.

Reality in God involves realizing our intimate co-inherence in God and in all creation. Ultimate human reality is not found to be an isolated or a collective ego. Rather, it is found to be Thomas Merton's "graced nothing." When this is realized, we no longer see ourselves as cut off and ultimately impoverished, "outside" of God, compelled to construct a self. Instead we realize our richness and dignity "in" God's Body. We know and appreciate our diversity within a gifted unity that simply *is*. It cannot be "constructed," only appreciated and demonstrated. Then community is simply lived out, not engineered. We are free to attend authentically to the speck in our neighbor's eye that obscures this awareness (within the limits of our still shadowed existence in a fallen world).

It is not good enough to hold this view merely as a concept. It must be embodied in all that we are for it to be empowered. Christian contemplative tradition can be helpful in this embodiment. It deals with human development not in terms of blind feeling or intellectual concept, but of carefully discerned intuitive realization that cuts a subtle path between intellect and feeling. Such realization frees both mind and feeling to be *servants* of such deeper awareness, rather than confused and competitive masters.

The rise of interest in this tradition at an experiential level today, seen through such practices as meditation, retreats, quiet prayer, and spiritual direction, is no accident. It follows an instinct of our nature that we are forever outside if we approach reality with our minds alone, and we are forever blind if we trust our waves of feeling without interior discernment.

The radical and energetic activity of many Christian contemplatives historically and today puts the lie to those who would dismiss such a tradition as passive and escapist of social reality. On the contrary, its attentiveness to a full simple embodiment of reality in God's wise compassion and a shedding of false self *frees* action that is likely to be in touch with the leading of the Spirit.

There is no guarantee of this, of course. Sin and blindness relentlessly remain latent with us. But I think authentic contemplative life does cultivate on-target vision and action. In any case, these years ahead need to foster contemplative awareness with ever greater care, and do so in the context of the church's full ministry and mission in the world. That is a major task to which I and Shalem are centrally committed. If it is neglected, the church risks continuing the bitter fruit of that neglect declared by Alan Watts many years ago: a fall either into literalist fundamentalism or into reductionist political movements that deny the full, subtle unity in diversity that life *is* in God.

The Generosity of God's Grace

Liberal Christian tradition has been very attentive to the Holy Spirit at work in the social and political movements of the world. It has often been much more tentative about seeing or caring about the Spirit at work in other deep religious traditions. On this subject the gap often is not operationally great between liberal and conservative Christians.

Perhaps there is a certain inevitability about this. The strong tendency to religious imperialism in Christian history, together with the tacit sense of competition and challenge from another religious way, leads even many liberal Christians to be more likely to see the Spirit in some form of contemporary psychological or political development than in the experience of another deep religious tradition.

At the same time it is worth noting the increasing number of probes in this direction.

The clearest probe of course continues to be across faith traditions *within* the Christian fold. The line between most Roman Catholics and Protestants is infinitely thinner now than it was twenty years ago. More openness to learn across the lines of Eastern and Western church traditions also is becoming apparent and important. The Eastern churches on the whole have a more intuitive/contemplative appreciation of life and the gospel that was passed down from the early church. Finally, appreciation across formal and more spontaneous liturgical lines has grown through a variety of mutual influences. All these mutually enriching and broadening traditions hopefully will continue to serve informal Christian unity.

Beyond this inter-Christian ecumenism there has been a dramatic rapprochement with Jewish tradition, which I hope will continue despite the pullbacks that recent trends toward harder ethnic lines has encouraged. With Jews there is a special sense of brother/sisterhood, of shared historic roots, and, for Christians, continued guilt over the pogroms that have denied that relationship. With Jews there also is healthy mutual challenge. Having lived in polarization for so long, blind spots, distortions, and ignorance of the grace given through one another's heritage are rife. Being together in a constructive way can lead us to be a mutual blessing for one another, as surely God intended it.

In the decade ahead we certainly will be gaining a broader knowledge of Muslim tradition, given our increasingly intimate involvement with Muslim nations and the growing number of university academic chairs and other centers that focus on Muslim cultures, along with the presence of a great many Muslim students in the West. For Christians unfamiliar with Islam it can come as quite a surprise to realize that Muslims accept both the Old and the New Testaments as part of their faith.

However, our political tensions with many of these nations, together with the Fundamentalist forms of Muslim life so visible to Westerners through recent events in Iran, do not provide a warm psychological climate for positive mutual learning. I hope this will not provide a long-term barrier, though, for Islam has great riches to share, especially, for me, in its Sufi mystical strain.

Arnold Toynbee long ago predicted that the confrontation of Buddhism with Christianity would be one of the most important and creative meeting grounds of the late twentieth century. Though such a prediction seems exaggerated in the face of so many other important meeting grounds that have emerged, for me personally it has proven to be true. I and many others I know continue to find special depth, precision, and challenge in the best of the Buddhist tradition that dramatically assists an opening up to the fullness of Christ, especially in terms of contemplative awareness. I think that the thousands of years of Buddhist attention to the mind's subtle states of awareness can do more for our opening than most contemporary psychologies combined.

But again at its best, it is a most profound tradition, and we will not find its depth from any brief encounter. The Christian-Buddhist meeting needs to be ongoing, and primarily on a shared experiential rather than simply conceptual level. The growing cross-fertilization of Christian and Buddhist contemplative communities and individuals will continue to prove a natural meeting ground.

The varied riches of Hindu, Taoist, African, Native American, and other religious traditions could be added to this list of places God's grace has been bestowed. Each of these would reflect ways that grace has been twisted or incomplete, as well, as we see in the Christian or any other tradition. What I am concerned about, though, is what each might contribute to confirm, challenge, and expand toward its fullness our understanding and experience of Christ. If Christians are to embody a truly universal faith, then it must account for the fullness of God's grace in the world. If we do not, then we have sold out to a stunted and sectarian faith that divides and constrains the fullness of the cosmic Christ whose Body fills all time and space. Christian contribution to the human family in the years ahead will suffer accordingly.

Krister Stendahl of the Harvard Divinity School recently prophesied the need and growth of a more inclusive theological language that can accommodate our growing mutual respect and learning across faith lines (as well as across masculine-feminine lines). Such language need not destroy the unique testimony of a given tradition; indeed, it can make that testimony more available to others. That is the historic task of Christian apologetics.

Such apologetics now, though, must ever further involve a two-way street with another tradition, a motive of sensitive Christian missions for some time. The goal should not be a constructed eclecticism any more than the old goal of a unilateral imperialism of narrowly defined Christian faith. Rather it should be a faith far richer and broader in its understanding of Jesus' words: "I am the way, and the truth, and the life" (John 14:6).

The Rhythm of Christian Life

Reestablishing an authentic rhythm between sabbath and ministry times is, perhaps, the church's most singularly important task on a mass scale in the decade ahead. I make such a bold statement because of the many rich contributions I am convinced this rhythm has to make to our time, and because of the unique position of the church in being able to understand and foster it. I have spoken to this rhythm only briefly in this book because I have given it so much attention elsewhere, not because of its relative unimportance.

Much experimentation in developing a viable corporate sabbath day is called for now, including rituals and practices that reveal its historic social vision, rest, worship, appreciation of creation, and joy. This is related to our capacity to foster genuine ministry time, which foundationally is an overflow of sabbath appreciation. Let me summarize and bring a step further its potential contributions.

Appreciation of Grace

In a compulsively production-oriented culture it is very difficult to live day by day with real attentiveness to grace. The cultural norms tempt us to flop back and forth between those two traps earlier mentioned that lie on each side of such attentive living. On one side is the pit of self-production. There we live the day as though we are completely on our own in a rather indifferent universe. It is up to us to produce an identity, a livelihood, hobbies, and the world. Feeling ourselves on our own, we have extremely high stakes in making it come out the way we want it. This orientation involves anxiety, attempts to control fully everything we can, and subtle violence toward anything that gets in our way. These are symptoms of idolatry. Idolatry comes easily when we feel ourselves so much on our own.

On the other side is the pit of passivity, or what historically would be called "sloth." There we live day by day as though God and everyone will take care of us and the world with no real cooperation on our part. We live in a kind of daily lethargy, a dulled, indifferent, evasive state marked by the easiest way we can get through the day.

A rhythm of sabbath and ministry time provides an antidote that helps us walk between these traps. Real sabbath time frees us to receptively notice the way life is gifted from the hand of God before and in our works. Compulsive productivity is loosened and made sane in work time. Such work becomes ministry when it is inspired by a vision of shalom. That vision is fleshed out and, in God's grace empowered, by the Christian sabbath. That sabbath carries a historical memory of our human calling to live with active attentiveness to the way we are meant to *be* grace for others, as they are for us; these are signs of God's reign—of shalom.

The potential contributions of this holy rhythm toward a correction of our insane cultural rhythm and views of self can be enormous and cumulative over time.

Endurance

The rhythm of sabbath and ministry has helped both Jews and Christians survive historically. Famous people in both traditions have questioned whether either tradition could survive without such a distinguishing rhythm. Probably no time in history has found that rhythm so neglected and threatened by cultural pressures.

The mainline established churches have been particularly negligent in understanding and attending this rhythm in recent decades. This I believe has seriously contributed to the erosion of their capacity to distinguish themselves by a way of life that does much more than echo the surrounding culture.

An authentic, shared rhythm of sabbath and ministry time can help save such churches and their members from being so much at the mercy of spiritually false cultural norms. A family, for example, that keeps a distinctively different quality of time on Sundays (without falling into old, repressive puritan habits), which in turn feeds a distinctive sense of ministry, will find that such a rhythm teaches a great deal about the Christian's two-edged vocation of resting in and serving the Lord. The rhythm itself witnesses to the gospel.

In a decade where adequate social vision is likely to be impeded by those who hold many of the world's reins of political, economic, and religious power, this sacred rhythm can help the socially concerned church endure without despair and capitulation. It is a rhythm that can bear us through the worst of times and provide perspective that again and again helps our discernment of what is important to attend.

This discernment can be enhanced and personalized by submitting to a discipline of spiritual direction with a soul friend, a subject addressed earlier. Such a discipline sits astride our sabbath and ministry time, helping us attend its particular called-for forms in our life at a given time.

Caring for a Shared Way of Life

I remember a Greek Orthodox scholar telling me once that it was completely impossible for a modern Western person to understand what community meant in the early centuries of the church. The sense of a communal way of life and values has been so diminished by the increasing individualism of the past several centuries that hardly any of us have the conditioning that would allow us to understand the nature of community for those ancestors in the faith.

Our individualism has been fed by an unprecedented historical experiment in pluralism. Even if our family, church, and ethnic groups retained some residual solidarity in a "way of life," our peek around the corner at other ways of life that are in effect taught as equally valid in school and law leaves us that much more on the edge of whatever way is ours.

When I look at the mixed-up-ness of my own background and experience, an inevitable streak of individualism comes to the fore. As I look back on my life, I see that a lot of confusion and cultural fragmentation also emerged. I see these realities more strongly than ever in those who are younger. Much creativity has emerged from both this individualism and these cultural conditions. But we cannot ignore the edge of social chaos to which they have brought us, nor the edge of ego-centered narcissism that so shrinks our called-for larger identity in God and creation and erodes authentic individualism. Individualism pushed beyond this larger context becomes a monstrous distortion of human calling and reality.

Such distortion is most apparent where cultural bonds have been loosened to the point of powerlessness. Perhaps we see this most clearly in parts of western states

like California where there has been little deep tradition
to give shape to individual life. Someone who does a
great deal of traveling around the country in his work
told me recently that he always feels most anxious when
he is in California. Why? "Because," he said, "I can't
predict what anyone is going to do. . . . There are so few
values held in common. . . . Anything goes. . . . Everyone's in their own private world. There is no distinction
between sanity and craziness."

Now this is an exaggeration, of course, and such
comments could be said with equal validity about many
other places (just as strong cultural bonds could be noted
in other parts of California). Nonetheless, I think his
feelings symbolize the outer edge of individualism we
have reached.

Liberals of the last several decades have, I think, paid
incredibly little attention to this general anxiety of
millions of people. In their orgy of concern for freeing
everyone from virtually any kind of cultural authority,
they have often forgotten that authentic individual
freedom and justice can exist only in the context of
commitment to an authentic society.

Such a society involves and rewards commitments to
social groupings that transcend the individual's direct,
immediate benefit: groupings that are familial, social,
religious, charitable, and political. An authentic society
also means commitment to a transcendent covenant
between all these groups and individuals that involves a
sense of vocation for the well-being of one another in the
nation, as well as for the whole planet (conservatives
usually fail this planetary test of authentic vision far
worse than liberals).

Such a situation calls for a clearer focus on cultural
reconstruction in the years ahead. This cannot be any
nostalgic revival of "the good old days," even if such days

ever really existed. The Spirit calls forth a unique pattern of living suitable for our time (though in continuity with fundamental structures of the past, such as a rhythm of sabbath and ministry time).

Such a reconstruction begins at home: in the way our household or other living community provides a way of life together in which we can share, a way that is not just "mine," but *ours*. Such a way needs to respect individual differences, but also needs to respect the social and divine identity that is part of a full human being.

We need to reestablish our confidence as cultural fathers and mothers, not just as privatized pals, friends, and single issue advocates. In the process, we need to avoid the rigidities and oversimplification of reality that come from fundamentalist attempts to father and mother a community, and the flabbiness of "anything goes as long as it doesn't directly hurt anyone." We are latent bearers of a massive historical and contemporary human experience and wisdom. We need to discern carefully what is worth passing on.

If we ignore this passing on, we leave others impoverished, ahistorical, pathetic creatures, easy prey of tyrants and private fantasy.

Such a discernment involves attention to our own "cultural enrichment." That phrase was used in the sixties for programs run by benighted middle-class folk for poor people. Today I think we are seeing the cumulative effects on the middle class of an educational and entertainment system that focuses on the technical and the informational, together with an eclectic, shallow, hodgepodge exposure to critical historical, social, religious, and artistic knowledge or commitment. Our resulting impoverishment calls for attention to the cultivation of household and community study, dialogue, and evolving norms that can aim at better equipping us for the kind of discernment that we are called upon to make and the kind of cultural depth and commitment we need, at many levels in our daily lives.

Gandhi was once allegedly asked, "What is civilization?" His response, in effect, was that it exists where people are conditioned to a postponement of gratification. When consequently asked about Western civilization, his answer was, "What civilization?"

Now this is clearly a gross exaggeration of our situation. But it does hold up a vital ingredient that is never missing from a society that caringly endures: the willingness to subsume immediate pleasure and ease to a deeper purpose—our hard exploration, attentiveness, and responsiveness to God's mysterious way for us. A rhythm of sabbath and ministry helps save this approach from being an overly tense affair that misses our call to "easeful mirth." But six-sevenths of our time in this yet-unfulfilled world is a call to face discerningly into the hard edges of life that seem to resist God's light except through our creative, knowledgeable fortitude.

14

The Sound Eye

I have reached this ending at the beginning of the church year. Advent began today: the season of hope for the wholeness of life in God. It is an important season, because it reminds us of the limits of our human vision and the fullness of God's empowered vision. Our own vision, unless inspirited by God's, is linear, narrow, and ultimately helpless. God's vision forever is breaking into such littleness with surprises.

The immediate impact of surprise is to leave us open and disarmed. For a flash we are cleansed of our own habits and free to be fully, awesomely present. After the flash, though, old habits easily return. Spiritual disciplines have the primary intent of conditioning us to remain longer in God's surprises, so that they have time to transform our vision into the one God has for us. Then we do not "return" to daily life quite so separated— rather, we find ourselves living a little more out of God. I have described for you some of the weighty Christian disciplines called for in our time. Together, in God's grace, such forms of attentiveness I believe can cultivate an integral, subtle way between all kinds of tempting destructive splits in the fabric of reality. We are called at our gifted best to live in reality "between" the splits, in that holy centering point where split-off fragments are changed from mutual contradiction into co-inherence, from gaping split into intimate, reconciled marriage.

This means living in the spacious connectedness *between* sexual, racial, social, national, and religious boundaries more deeply than we live within any particular one of these. It also means living in that sense of connectedness lying *between* a sense of self and other, *between* feelings, body, intuition, and intellect, *between* cultural accommodation and sectarian withdrawal, *between* sabbath and ministry, *between* eternity and history.

Between these is that "sound eye" of the body that Jesus says we need if the body is to be full of light and not darkness (Matt. 6:22). This eye is panoramic; it sees in all directions; it has the wide-eyed innocence of the first moment of surprise, before being clouded by our habits, fears, and grasping. It is this gifted eye that sees everything "inside," as connected, and as mysteriously transformed and endlessly upheld in the One who lives through me and you and all.

Finally, it is that inner eye that sees Merton's "graced nothing" at the bottom of every "thing"; no-*thing* leaves only the varyingly shaped openness of grace, the inspirited shared life that is the joy of God. This eye is embodied and resurrected for us in Jesus Christ. When it is clear, we are saved from falling into sin and confusion—into some willful or blind split-off "outsideness" that no longer knows the source of its life and real hope.

May that graced clarity, that empowered Presence become ever brighter in these years ahead among all God's children.